THOUGHTS ON THE PARASHA

BY

Rabbi Eliyahu Attias

ISBN 1-892692-40-6

Printed in the United States of America

Contents

Introduction

WITH DEEP GRATITUDE TO Hashem, I present this collection of insights on the weekly Parashah.

A milestone in Torah study is celebrated with a festive dinner, as the Midrash[1] learns from Shelomo HaMelech:

> In Givon, Hashem appeared to Shelomo in a dream of the night. God said to him, "Request what I should give to you."
>
> Shelomo said, "Grant Your servant an understanding heart...."
>
> God said to him, "...Behold, I have given you a wise and understanding heart...."
>
> Shelomo.... came to Jerusalem..., sacrificed burnt offerings and peace offerings, and made a banquet for all his servants.[2]

I fondly recall Simhat Torah in the Lakewood Yeshiva. By the time we finished all the day's prayers and *hakafot,* the sun had already set. Our Rosh Yeshiva, Rav Aharon Kotler *ztz"l,* urged us to eat a festive meal — not in honor of Yom Tov, since it was already after sunset, but in honor of completing the yearly cycle of the public Torah reading.

What exactly are we rejoicing over when we complete a milestone in Torah study? And how do we learn to make a festive dinner from Shelomo? His banquet was made before he had completed anything!

I suggest one answer to both questions. Shelomo HaMelech

---

1. *Kohelet Rabbah* 1:1.
2. Melachim 1 3:5–15.

rejoiced at having received wisdom with which to understand Hashem's Torah, His mitzvot, and His creation. When we complete a Talmudic tractate, we rejoice at having acquired familiarity with its principles and laws, which will enable us to learn it better next time. And on Simhat Torah, we rejoice at having acquired the background for deepening our understanding of the weekly Parashah in the coming year.

Indeed, as we go through the weekly Parshah again each year, we can and should delve deeper and deeper into it.

The story is told of a man who brought his eight-year-old grandson to the rabbi and said proudly, "This child understands Humash and Rashi as well as I do."

"It's wonderful that the child understands Torah like the grandfather," said the rabbi. "But how unfortunate that the grandfather understands Torah like the child!"

Vayeshev

SEEKING TRANQUILITY

Yaakov settled in the land of his father's sojourning, in the Land of Canaan. (Bereshit 37:1.)

After his ordeals with Lavan, Esav, and Shechem, Yaakov wished to settle down in tranquility. Instead, he was hit with a new ordeal: the disappearance of Yoseph.

The Midrash[1] comments:

When the righteous dwell in tranquility and seek to dwell in tranquility in this world, Hashem says, "Isn't what awaits the righteous in the world to come enough for them? Why should they seek to dwell in tranquility in this world?"[2]

We know that this is so because Yaakov Avinu sought to dwell in tranquility in this world and the anguish of Yoseph came to him. *Yaakov settled* — "I was not tranquil, I was not quiet, and I was not at rest, and torment came."[3] "I was not tranquil" — from Esav, "I was not quiet" — from Lavan, "I was not at rest" — from Dinah, "and torment came" — the torment of Yoseph came upon me.

---

1. *Bereshit Rabbah.*
2. According to a different version, it is Satan who says this
3. Iyov 3:25.

This Midrash is puzzling from the very first line. What is meant by "the righteous dwell in tranquility and seek to dwell in tranquility"? If they are already dwelling in tranquility, why do they need to seek it? Besides, how can the Midrash make such a generalization? Many tzaddikim live in ease in this world. Even Yaakov did so during the fourteen years he spent in the yeshiva of Shem and Ever and during the seventeen years he spent in Egypt at the end of his life.

We can explain this by picturing a gym with various exercise machines. Some strengthen the back, others the stomach, legs, and neck. The coach assigns to each person the particular machine he needs to strengthen his weak muscles.

This world is a "gym" for strengthening character traits. One person needs to tone up his patience, a second his humility, a third his trust in Hashem. Each is assigned the "exercise machines" on which he needs to work out in order to strengthen his weak traits.

Knowing this principle, the tzaddik remains serene when he faces a tough ordeal. He isn't broken; he doesn't become sad or depressed. He is like the person working out on a treadmill. It's hard and he sweats; but he is happy, knowing that the workout will make him stronger, and he even enjoys it.

This aptly describes Yaakov. Before his death, he looked back at his trouble-filled life and said, "God, Who has shepherded me from my inception until this day...."[4] A shepherd leads his sheep to the places that are best for them, where they will have food and drink. Yaakov truly felt that Hashem had arranged all the events of his life for his benefit, to raise him to spiritual heights.

So the tzaddik is always in a state of tranquility, even when

---

4. Bereshit 48:16.

troubles beset him. Why, then, does the Midrash say that he also wants a state of tranquility?

The tzaddik wants an easy life because that is also an ordeal! As *Mesilat Yesharim* says in the first chapter:

> All worldly matters, whether good or bad, are trials for a person — poverty on one hand, and wealth on the other,... tranquility on the one hand and suffering on the other, so that a person is under attack from all sides.

In fact, of all trials, tranquility is the most difficult to pass. For when Hashem pampers us, we tend to forget Him.[5]

When Yaakov came back to the Land of Israel, he wanted the most difficult trial.

In response, Hashem said, "Isn't what awaits the righteous in the world to come enough for them? Why do they seek to dwell in tranquility in this world?" The tzaddik can determine his situation and level in the world to come; these are entirely in his hands. But his situation in this world is determined by Hashem; it's like the gym, where the coach assigns specific machines for each client to work out on.

This explains why there are other tzaddikim without the troubles of Yaakov. Each person has his own custom-tailored workout program in this world. For instance, to one Hashem may give many children; to another, none. Both situations are trials.

Mesilat Yesharim ends the chapter:

> *Thus we learn* that a person exists in this world mainly to fulfill mitzvot, *laavod* — to work, and to withstand tests.

Thus we learn — where in this chapter did *Mesilat Yesharim*

---

5. See Hovot HaLevavot, Shaar HaBitahon, ch. 3.

teach this? And what is meant by *laavod* — to work? What work is a major purpose of our existence?

Perhaps this refers to the very beginning of the chapter:

> The foundation of piety and the root of perfect *avodah* ("service" or "work"), is that it should become clear and true to a person what his duty in his world is.

When we suffer, we naturally turn to Hashem and remember what He requires of us. When we have it easy, we tend to forget; the work then is much more challenging. Both in easy times and in rough times, our *avodah* is to remember what we are here for.

YOSEPH AND HIS BROTHERS

> *...Yoseph would bring evil reports about [his brothers] to their father, [telling him that the brothers ate limbs from living animals, slighted the sons of the maidservants by calling them servants, and were suspected of immorality.[6]]*
>
> *Yisrael loved Yoseph more than all his sons since he was a ben zekunim to him, and he made him a ketonet passim.[7] His brothers saw that his father loved him... so they hated him; and they could not speak to him peaceably.*
>
> *Yoseph dreamt a dream. He told his brothers, and they hated him even more. He said to them, "Hear, now, this dream that I dreamt."* (Bereshit 37:2–6.)

Why did Yaakov make Yoseph a *ketonet passim,* thereby causing jealousy? And when Yoseph saw that his brothers hated him and didn't return his greetings, why did he add fuel to the fire by telling them his dreams?

---

6. Rashi.
7. Fine woolen tunic.

The Midrash[8] provides a clue: When Yoseph said to them, "Hear, now, this dream that I dreamt," he meant to say, "This is how the prophets will rebuke you, saying, — "Hear, now, the word of Hashem.'"

Thus we see that Yoseph was a prophet. Perhaps he foresaw prophetically that exile was imminent and the decree that "your offspring shall be aliens in a land not their own"[9] would soon be fulfilled. Yoseph thought that they needed to prepare for exile and make rules to protect Yaakov's family from assimilation in the foreign land.

Yoseph when he brought the "evil reports" — that the brothers ate limbs from living animals, slighted the sons of the maidservants by calling them servants, and were suspected of immorality — was actually consulting with Yaakov about protective rules concerning these three problem areas. Yoseph wished to institute "fences" in three areas that protect the Jewish people to this day. He established:

Kashrut. "You shall distinguish between the clean animal and the unclean.... You shall be holy unto Me... I have separated you from the nations to be Mine."[10] Therefore eat in a refined, dignified, holy way. Don't grab and eat quickly. Meat should be eaten only after considerable preparation.

Unity. Don't look down at fellow Jews. Live in harmony. In unity there is strength.

Holiness. Be holy in matters of morality. Guard your eyes against forbidden sights.

Yaakov agreed to these three fences, and he made Yoseph a garment of distinction to show that he was appointing Yoseph as *Mashgiah* — ethical counselor — of his brothers. Being a *ben zekunim*

---

8. *Bereshit Rabbah* 4:10.
9. Bereshit 15:13.
10. End of Parashat Kedoshim, Vayikra 20:25 –26.

to Yaakov made Yoseph the most suitable for this function.

What is a *ben zekunim*? Some translate "a child of his old age." But Yoseph was not the youngest, he had a younger brother: Binyamin.

Our Sages explain *ben zekunim* to mean that Yoseph looked like Yaakov[11] and that Yaakov taught Yoseph the Torah he had learned in the yeshiva of Shem and Ever.[12]

The Midrash adds: Whatever befell Yaakov also befell Yoseph. Each had been born to a mother who had been barren until then, and then gave birth to two. Both their brothers sought to kill them. Each married outside of Eretz Yisrael. And the list continues.

What is the Midrash teaching us?

That the events in a person's life shape his character and prepare him to fulfill his mission. The events that built Yaakov into the greatest of the Forefathers also built Yoseph into the greatest of the brothers. Although Yaakov had not been born first, he became the firstborn of Yitzhak's family; and although Yoseph had not been born first, he, too, became the firstborn; the leader and director of Yaakov's family.

When the brothers refused to accept Yoseph's guidance, he had prophetic dreams. In the first one, their sheaves bowed down to his sheaf. He told the brothers, "Hashem agrees with me. He showed me in a dream that there will be a famine, we will go to a foreign land to obtain food, and you will need me for physical survival. Heed my words, for we must prepare for the upcoming exile."

In the second dream, heavenly bodies bowed down to Yoseph. He told the brothers, "This dream foretells that you will also need my guidance in spiritual matters."

The dreams were fulfilled twenty-two years later. Yaakov's

---

11. *Zekunim* is understood as a contraction of *ziv ikunim*, "countenance."
12. *Zekunim* is understood as a contraction of *zeh kanah hochmah*, "this one has accumulated wisdom."

family went down to Egypt, where Yoseph not only provided them with food but also advised them to live in the sector of Goshen and to be shepherds.

Evidently it was Yoseph who guided them to keep their own language, garments, and names during the exile, and in this merit they were eventually redeemed. When he revealed himself to his brothers, he said, "I am Yoseph",[13] using his Hebrew name — not "I am Tzofnat Paaneah"; and "Your eyes see... that my mouth is speaking to you [in the Holy Tongue].[14]

When he had the dreams at age seventeen, Yoseph intended only to be his brothers' guide and advisor. But the brothers misunderstood him thinking he wanted to rule over them, and strongly objected, saying, "Will you reign over us? Will you rule us?"[15]

The brothers had a point. Shemuel HaNavi,[16] too, would later object to the Jewish people's request for a king. For ideally, we should serve only one King — Hashem.

REUVEN'S REPENTANCE

The brothers put Yosef into a pit and then sold him without Reuven's knowledge. *Reuven returned to the pit — and behold, Yoseph was not in the pit! So he rent his garments.* (Bereshit 37:29)

We would have expected the verse to say, "Reuven came to the pit." "Reuven returned" implies that he had been involved in something else. In what? The answer is found in the very same words, "and he returned", he had been involved in *teshuvah,* returning to Hashem.

---

13. Bereshit 44:3.
14. Rashi Bereshit 45:12
15. Bereshit 37:8.
16. The prophet.

The Midrash[17] says:

> "Reuven returned." Where had he been? Rabbi Eliezer says he was involved with his sackcloth and fast. When he finished, he went and peered into the pit...
>
> Hashem said to him, "No person has ever before sinned before Me and done *teshuvah*. By your life, your descendant will be the first to speak of *teshuvah*."
>
> And who is that? Hoshea, who said, "Return, O Israel, to Hashem, your God."[18]

Why did Reuven decide to do *teshuvah* specifically now, during the sale of Yoseph?

And why does the Midrash say that Reuven was the first to repent? Adam and Cain had done so, long before! And why does it say that Hoshea was the first prophet to call for repentance? Many prophets had done so long before!

Evidently, Reuven's *teshuvah* was unique — and so was Hoshea's call for repentance.

In order to understand, let's back up a little. When the brothers wanted to kill Yoseph it says, "Reuven heard, and he saved him from their hand."[19]

What did Reuven do to save Yoseph? He told the brothers to throw Yoseph into a pit instead of killing him. But we know that the pit was full of snakes and scorpions![20] Can that be called saving him?

The *Zohar* explains that Reuven thought: If Yoseph falls into the hands of Shimon and Levi, nothing will be left of him. If he

---

17. *Bereshit Rabbah* 4:19.
18. Hoshea 14:2.
19. Bereshit 37:21.
20. Rashi, Bereshit 37:24.

dies in the pit, at least I'll return the body to our father [and he'll have a Jewish burial].

So when Reuven returned and found no trace of Yoseph either dead or alive, he immediately rent his garments.

Accordingly, we may say that Reuven obtained an important insight into human character.

The brothers had convened a *bet din*,[21] deliberated gravely, and ruled that Yoseph was a *rodef* — one who is trying to kill someone — and thus deserves to be killed.

They judged him to be a *rodef* because he had brought evil reports to their father accusing them of transgressing three grave sins. Thus the brothers might be cut off from the Jewish nation as Yitzhak's sinful son Esav had been. Or Yoseph might convince Yaakov that the nation be built only from Rachel's sons and the brothers might be cut off just as Avraham's sons by Hagar and Keturah had been. Since the brothers did not believe that Yoseph's dreams were prophetic, the brothers' decision seemed reasonable and justified.

However, when "Reuven heard" them speak of ripping Yoseph to pieces, he realized that hatred and anger had welled up inside them causing them to stop thinking logically, lose control of themselves, and do unthinkable deeds.

Seeing this happen to the brothers, Reuven began to reflect on his own sin.

After Rahel died, Reuven expected Yaakov to move into the tent of his mother, Leah. Instead, Yaakov moved into the tent of Rahel's maidservant, Bilhah. Reuven was jealous for his mother's honor, and he thought his father had erred. Although it is wrong to think this about the greatest of the Forefathers, whose image

---

21. Court.

is carved beneath the heavenly throne, and even Reuven probably thought that there was some justification, however, jealousy welled up in Reuven until he stopped thinking logically, lost control, and did the unthinkable act of tampering with his father's bedroom.

Now Reuven realized that he too allowed jealousy and anger to well up until he lost control of himself. So he repented not just for the act itself but also for the jealousy and anger that were the cause of his sin.

This same point was later made by the prophet Hoshea, who proclaimed, "Return, O Israel, to Hashem, your God" — You claim that you had logical reasons for doing what you did. Will you use the same self-justification when you face Hashem, Who sees into your mind and heart and knows the truth? Or will you have to admit that you let jealousy and anger well up until you lost control?

Adam and Cain repented for known sins, and theirs was the type of repentance of which the other prophets spoke. But Hoshea said, "Return... for you stumbled in your iniquity" — repent for having lost control of yourselves and gone beyond the bounds of reason.

Human nature hasn't changed. Today, too, a person sometimes loses his temper and with it his reason and self-control. Afterwards, when he calms down, he asks himself, "How could I have said what I said? How could I have done what I did?"

Hoshea teaches us to always ask ourselves: Will my self-justification hold up when I come before Hashem?

PARASHAT

$\mathcal{M}$iketz

YOSEPH'S TRUST IN HASHEM

Yoseph had been in prison for twelve years when he interpreted the dream of the chamberlain of the cupbearers telling him that he would be released from prison and restored to his position. He then asked the chamberlain to remember him and vouch for him to Pharaoh. Yosef said to [the chamberlain of the cupbearers] *"Remember me with yourself... and mention me to Pharaoh...."*

But the chamberlain of the cupbearers did not remember Yoseph, and he forgot him.

It came to pass at the end of two years to the day: Pharaoh was dreaming... (Bereshit 40:12– 41:1)

Says the Midrash,[1] "Praiseworthy is the man who made Hashem his trust and turned not to the arrogant"[2] refers to Yoseph. Because he said to the chamberlain of the cupbearers, *Remember me with yourself... and mention me to Pharaoh...,* two years were added to his prison term.

Why does the Midrash contradict itself, praising Yoseph for his trust in Hashem and at the same time criticizing him for asking the chamberlain for help?

Furthermore, what was wrong with saying two words to the

---

1. *Bereshit Rabbah* 9:3.
2. Tehilim 40: 5.

11

chamberlain? *Hovot HaLevavot*[3] says that Hashem wants a person to do a little *hishtadlut;*[4] it's a mitzvah to make some effort. True, Rabbi Shimon bar Yohai maintains that men should study Torah full time and rely on Hashem to provide for them. But even he wasn't against a small *hishtadlut,* such as taking a tenant farmer to work one's fields. And Yoseph's *hishtadlut* was miniscule — two words to the chamberlain!

Perhaps we can explain in light of another point from *Hovot HaLevavot:*[5] Our *hishtadlut* has no effect whatsoever! The outcome is in Hashem's hands alone. Success and failure are not related to effort.

In order to teach us this, Hashem will sometimes make a surefire *hishtadlut* fail. Then we see that it is not our effort but Hashem's decree that causes the outcome.

Now let's look at a fuller section of the Tehilim[6] from which the Midrash quoted.

> *I have greatly hoped for Hashem.... He raised me from a pit....*
>
> *Praiseworthy is the man who made Hashem his trust, and turned not to the arrogant....*
>
> *For innumerable troubles have encircled me.... My enemies say...,*
> *"When will he die and his name perish?"...Even my ally in whom I trusted, who ate my bread, has raised his heel against me.*
>
> *But You, Hashem, show me favor and raise me up, and I shall repay them.*

"I shall repay them"? Surely a tzaddik does not take revenge! What does David HaMelech mean?

---

3. *Shaar HaBitahon.*
4. Effort.
5. *Shaar HaBitahon.*
6. Chapters 40–41.

A tzaddik "falls seven times and rises."[7] David fell into a pit and continued to fall deeper and deeper, seven times. Instead of helping him, his enemies cursed him. Even a friend to whom he had served dinner kicked him.[8]

When David rose, he paid them back — not with bad, but with good![9] For he understood that their harsh treatment of him was decreed by Hashem and was for his own benefit.

This attitude can be illustrated by the following parable.

Hayyim went for a massage and took his friend Dov along. Poor Dov didn't know what was in store for him. The masseur made him lie on a bed and started kneading his stomach as if it were dough. Then he twisted his arm and pulled his legs. When Hayyim handed the torturer a bribe, Dov hoped it would lead to kinder treatment; instead, the masseur used even more energy.

The two friends finished their massage sessions and walked out together. "How did you like it?" asked Hayyim.

"I'm dizzy," said Dov, panting and limping. "I can barely walk."

"Really?" said Hayyim in surprise. "I feel wonderful!"

David HaMelech also felt wonderful and said, "All my suffering was for my own benefit. The ally whom I trusted didn't help me — so that I would learn that my *hishtadlut* accomplishes nothing." And instead of becoming angry at the ally, David gave him gifts of gratitude for the lesson.

Yoseph, too, was kicked by his ally. He asked the chamberlain, for whom he had done many favors, to help him — but the chamberlain didn't.

The Midrash relates that the chamberlain would tie knots on his hand to remind him to mention Yoseph to Pharaoh. Perhaps

---

7. Mishlei 24:16.
8. See Radak.
9. Radak, citing Rabbenu Saadyah Gaon.

that is the meaning of Yoseph's request, "Remember me with you."
Make a reminder that is with you —a thread tied on your hand.

But, continues the Midrash, an angel would come and untie
the threads. They kept falling off, and the chamberlain simply
could not remember.

Two years later, when Pharaoh dreamt his dream, the chamberlain finally remembered. But now, he did not want to help
Yoseph; he had turned into an enemy. "Even my ally in whom I
trusted, who ate my bread, has raised his heel against me."

The chamberlain waited and waited until Pharaoh almost died
of distress. Then he thought: I can't let Pharaoh die — his successor is liable to give my position to one of his own men!

So he went to Pharaoh and began, "Today I am mentioning
my sins"[10] — plural. There were two sins: forgetting Yoseph and
letting Pharaoh suffer so long.

With this, Hashem wanted to teach Yoseph, and all of us,
one last lesson before catapulting him overnight from the low-
est depths to the highest heights: *Hishtadlut* is not what brings
results!

Yoseph learned the lesson. After Hashem turned him overnight from an imprisoned slave into a powerful viceroy, he never
took revenge against the chamberlain. He knew that it wasn't the
chamberlain's fault.

Actually, Yoseph had never "turned" to the chamberlain. When
he said, *Remember me with yourself... and mention me*, it was only
to fulfill the will of Hashem, Who commanded us to do a little
hishtadlut. Yoseph always put his trust only in Hashem — to such
an extent that our Sages said of him, "Praiseworthy is the man who
made Hashem his trust."

---

10. Bereshit 41:9.

What proof is there that Yoseph made Hashem his trust?

Hovot HaLevavot[11] says that a person who has *bitahon* will always have *menuhat hanefesh,* peace of mind, because he knows that Hashem is watching over him and doing only good for him.

If so, we can easily check Yoseph's *bitahon.* We need only check his state of mind after ten years in the dungeon with no prospects of ever getting out.

We see Yoseph asking the two chamberlains, "Why are your faces downcast today?"[12] — Even if you are prisoners in the dungeon, you should smile.

Then we see him interpreting their dreams through Divine inspiration, which rests only at a person who has *simhah*[13] and peace of mind.

How could Yoseph smile under such dreadful circumstances? There is only one possible answer: He had perfect *bitahon.*

PHARAOH'S DREAM

After Yosef interpreted Pharaoh's dream, telling him that there would be seven years of plenty followed by seven years of famine Yosef said, *"Now let Pharaoh seek out a discerning and wise man, and set him over the land of Egypt."* (Bereshit 41:33)

After interpreting Pharaoh's dream, why did Yoseph go on to give Pharaoh advice? Who asked for his opinion? How dared he imply that Pharaoh couldn't take care of matters himself? And why did he suggest that Pharaoh appoint an outsider, rather than one of his own advisors?

---

11. *Shaar HaBitahon.*
12. Bereshit 40:7.
13. Joy.

Let's look for answers in the verses themselves.

Earlier in the chapter, Pharaoh related his dream to Yoseph and concluded: "I told the sorcerers [my dream], but no one could tell me [the interpretation]."[14] There is a question implied here: Why did the sorcerers, who usually interpret dreams well, miss the mark?

In fact, we find that Yoseph began answering this implied question even before hearing the dream, for Yoseph's first words to Pharaoh were "God will respond with Pharaoh's welfare and peace"[15] — Hashem wants Pharaoh to know the future for the sake of Pharaoh's welfare and peace. Therefore the dream came in metaphors that the sorcerers couldn't interpret, and therefore Hashem wanted to put an outsider in charge, because although Pharaoh's men are wise, that isn't enough, the appointee must also be discerning and know the tricks of storing wheat so that it won't spoil. The people's complaints will be directed to this appointee, and Pharaoh will not have *shalom,* peace, from complaints and blame.

Indeed, when the famine came and the people cried out to Pharaoh, he told them, "Go to Yoseph."[16]

So now Yoseph said, "...let Pharaoh seek out a discerning and wise man, and set him over the land of Egypt," for the sake of *shelom Pharaoh.*

Pharaoh figured: If Yoseph knew in advance that the dream pertained to my welfare, he must be "a man who has in him the spirit of God"[17] — a man with Divine inspiration, and he is the one I'll appoint.

14. Bereshit 41:24.
15. Bereshit 41:16.
16. Bereshit 41:55.
17. Bereshit 41:38.

But why did Pharaoh bring in Yoseph to begin with? What made him reject his sorcerers' interpretations — such as, "You will beget seven daughters and bury seven daughters"?

Siftei Hachamim explains that dreams of kings do not pertain to their private matters, only to matters of their kingdom or the world.

If so, why did Pharaoh reject his sorcerers' interpretation that "You will conquer seven kingdoms, and seven kingdoms will rebel against you"[18]?

We may explain as follows. The word *Mitzrayim*[19] translated literally means, "two banks" because it is located on both banks of the Nile, the source of Egypt's sustenance. Pharaoh dreamt that he was standing on the bank of the Nile because as the head of state, he was responsible for the people's sustenance.

Pharaoh understood that this point was the essence of his dream. The proof is that he told Yoseph, "In my dream, behold! I was standing on the bank of the Nile."[20]

Pharaoh rejected the sorcerers' interpretations because only Yoseph's interpretation dealt with sustenance.

THE VICEROY MAKES DEMANDS

All the land of Egypt hungered. The people cried out to Pharaoh for bread. Pharaoh said to all of Egypt, "Go to Yoseph. Do whatever he tells you." (Bereshit 41:55)

Rashi explains that Pharaoh told the Egyptians to listen to Yoseph who had told the Egyptians to circumcise themselves.

---

18. *Bereshit Rabbah* 89:6.
19. Egypt.
20. Bereshit 48:17.

Why would Yoseph want them to do so? After all, the Jews would soon be exiled to Egypt, wouldn't it be better if the gentiles were not circumcised so that they would be set apart from the gentiles through circumcision, just as they would be set aside by their clothing, their names, and their language?

We find a clue in the Midrash,[21] which relates that when the Egyptians cried out to Pharaoh, he asked them, "Why didn't you store grain?"

"We did," they replied, "but it all rotted, and so did the bread we baked."

Pharaoh sent them to Yoseph, who told them, "My God does not feed the uncircumcised. Go circumcise yourself, and I will give you grain."

What did Yoseph mean by "My God does not feed the uncircumcised?" Doesn't Hashem feeds all of mankind, circumcised or not?

The answer is found in the same Midrash. The fact that all the grain rotted except for the grain of Yoseph showed that Hashem was not sustaining the world naturally as He does in normal times, rather, He was granting sustenance only miraculously in the merit of Yoseph HaTzaddik.

If so, the grain was not natural — it was miraculous and holy, and should not be given to people who had the disgrace[22] of a foreskin.

This idea sheds light on the end of our Parshah. Yoseph's brothers "were frightened when they were brought to Yoseph's house. They said, 'We are being brought... because of the money replaced in our sacks... to take us as slaves along with our donkeys.'"[23]

---

21. *Bereshit Rabbah* 91:5.
22. As Shimon and Levi called it; see Bereshit 34:14.
23. Bereshit 43:18.

If a person is frightened about being pressed into slavery, does he worry about his donkey?

We may answer that these donkeys, owned as they were by tzaddikim, were connected to holiness — like Rabbi Pinhas ben Yair's donkey, which refused to eat untithed grain. The brothers did not want such donkeys to fall into the hands of gentiles, and they were happy when their donkeys were saved, as the verse points out, "The day dawned, and the men were sent off, they and their donkeys."[24]

Similarly, the *Yerushalmi* relates that a gentile once bought an ox from a Jew, and when Shabbat came, the ox refused to work.

The Ben Ish Hai[25] teaches that any physical object that was used to serve something or someone holy acquires an element of holiness itself. Thus our Sages said that the rock on which Rabbi Eliezer ben Horkenos sat when he learned Torah resembled Mount Sinai. A prophet's walking stick, on which he would lean when having holy intents, also acquired holiness.

By sanctifying himself, Yoseph brought sustenance and sanctity to the world. Even on our level, when we sanctify ourselves, we bring blessing and generate sanctity, which spreads out to the world — to people, animals, plants, and even inanimate objects.

ACCUSED OF ESPIONAGE

When the brothers descended to Egypt and presented themselves to Yosef, *Yoseph remembered the dreams that he had dreamed about them, and he said to them, "You are spies!"* (Bereshit 42:9.)

How could Yoseph accuse his brothers of espionage? Surely he knew that the Torah forbids taking revenge!

---

24. Bereshit 43:3
25. *Ben Yehoyada, Sanhedrin* 95a.

The *Zohar*[26] answers: Yoseph never sought revenge. He called them spies only to force them to bring Binyamin, whom he longed for.

This answer demands explanation. Surely Yoseph would not cause his brothers anguish just so that he could see Binyamin!

We may explain that Yoseph wanted to remove any trace of resentment from his heart and replace it with love. He figured that seeing his brother Binyamin, who had not been involved in selling him into slavery, would arouse his love for the whole family, which it, in fact, did, for at the sight of Binyamin, Yoseph was so elated and moved that he went into his private room and wept, and then invited the brothers to dine with him.

In light of this, we can understand the connection between the two parts of the verse: "Yoseph remembered the dreams," and, "he said to them, 'You are spies!'"

To Yoseph, even more painful than being sold into slavery was being misunderstood — which caused the rift. As we explained in Parashat Vayeshev, Yoseph tried to guide the brothers to prepare for the upcoming exile by sanctifying themselves and uniting, and their father designated Yoseph as the family's Mashgiah, making him a garment of distinction to show it. Yoseph then told them his dreams to show that Hashem wanted them to accept his guidance. But they misinterpreted Yoseph's intentions and accused him of trying to rule over them.

Now "Yoseph remembered the dreams that he had dreamed for them, and he said to them, 'You are spies!'" It says, "for them," for the dreams had indeed been for their benefit. In order to replace his bad feelings with love, Yoseph called them spies in order that they should bring Binyamin.

---

26. Page 199.

Later, Yoseph would tell them, "Behold, your eyes see as do the eyes of my brother Binyamin that it is my mouth that is speaking to you."[27] Rashi comments:

> He set them all equal to one another, to say: Just as I have no hatred in my heart toward my brother Binyamin, who had no part in selling me, so too, I have no hatred in my heart toward you.

THE SILVER GOBLET

When the brothers left Yosef they were chased by Yosef's agents who accused them of stealing his goblet. The brothers said, *Anyone among your servants with whom it is found shall die.* (Bereshit 44:9)

The brothers said this when Yoseph's messenger caught up with them and accused them of stealing his silver goblet. Little did they know that the goblet had been planted in Binyamin's satchel.

How could the brothers risk saying that whoever had the goblet would die — especially after money was planted in their satchels on their first trip to Egypt? Why didn't they suspect that the goblet, too, had been planted?

Perhaps they thought that the money was planted by a petty clerk in order to frame them, but no one could plant the goblet which never left the hand of the viceroy; and they didn't suspect the viceroy of doing so.

To their dismay, they soon discovered that the viceroy had done exactly that, in order to retain Binyamin.

Yoseph did other strange things as well — all carefully designed to help the brothers realize that they had been mistaken.

When the brothers first came to Egypt, Yosef falsely accused

---

27. Bereshit 45:12.

them of espionage, saying, "You are spies" — *rodfim*[28] bent on destroying Egypt. This was a hint: Hadn't they, too, once falsely accused someone of being a *rodef*?

This time too, he invited them to a meal and tapping his goblet as if divining, he called out their names, seating them by age, and putting Binyamin closest to him. This, too, was a hint: Perhaps Yoseph's dreams were prophetic?

Yoseph repeatedly prompted the brothers to see their mistakes so that they would repent. Now, as in his youth, he tried to guide them to higher levels of righteousness.

---

28. Pursuers.

Vayigash

CONFRONTATION

After Yosef accused Binyamin of stealing the goblet, *Yehudah approached [Yoseph] and said...* (Bereshit 44:18)

The Midrash[1] applies a passage from Tehilim[2] to this confrontation between Yehudah and the viceroy of Egypt:

"For behold the kings assembled, they were angered[3] together." Yehudah and Yoseph were angry at one another.

"They saw and were really astounded." The other brothers were astounded, as it is written, *"[The brothers] looked at one another in astonishment."*[4]

"Trembling gripped them there." This refers to the brothers. They said, "Kings are quarreling with each other. As for us, what do we care? It is appropriate for a king to quarrel with a king."

Then the Midrash applies a passage from Iyov:[5]

"One approaches the other." This refers to Yehudah and Yoseph.

---

1. *Bereshit Rabbah* 93:2.
2. Tehilim 48:5–7.
3. The Midrash understands *avru* (עברו) here as related to *evrah* (עברה), "wrath."
4. Bereshit 43:33.
5. Iyov 41:8.

The brothers said, "Kings are quarreling with each other. As for us, what do we care?"

How could the brothers say, "What do we care?" Surely they cared about Binyamin being taken as a slave, not to mention the anguish this would cause their father! Besides, the Midrash itself proves that they cared — by quoting the verse "Trembling gripped them there."

We can explain in light of the verse, "He who becomes angry[6] over a dispute that is not his is like the one who seizes a dog's ears."[7] Rashi explains that the dog will bite him. He thought he would control the situation by seizing the dog's ears but instead he got into trouble with the dog. Similarly, a bystander who enters a conflict will only make matters worse. Instead of two people quarreling, there will now be three, and the conflict will spread.

When the brothers saw the dispute between Yehudah and Yoseph, they were so involved emotionally that trembling gripped them. But they knew that the Torah outlook required them to put their mind in charge of their feelings and stay out of the dispute. So they said, "What do we care?"

This teaches us an important lesson.

When our Torah authorities disagree, the people around them must say, "What do we care?" Our Torah giants are kings, as our Sages said, "Who are kings? The Torah scholars." "It is appropriate for a king to quarrel with a king" — it is appropriate for *gedolim*[8] to debate an issue, since they understand it in depth, but we do not.

So when two *gedolim* disagree, ordinary people have no business mixing in. Whoever mixes in, is putting himself in danger,

---

6. *Over mit'aber.*
7. Mishlei 26:17.
8. Torah giants.

like the man who seized the dog's ears, for Hashem defends the honor of Torah scholars.

YOSEPH REVEALS HIS IDENTITY

Yoseph said to his brothers, "I am Yoseph. Is my father still alive?"
And his brothers could not answer him because they were disconcerted before him. (Bereshit 45:3)

From the brothers' reaction, the Midrash[9] deduces that Yoseph's words were a scathing rebuke.

Abba Cohen Bardela said: Woe to us from the Day of Judgment! Woe to us from the Day of Rebuke!

Yoseph was the youngest of the brothers, yet they could not stand before his rebuke.... When Hashem comes and rebukes every single person according to what he is..., how much more so!

But all Yosef said was "I am Yoseph. Is my father still alive?" Where is the rebuke?

The *Bet HaLevi* answers: These few words refuted all of Yehudah's arguments. When Yoseph declared that he was taking Binyamin as a slave, Yehudah asked to take Binyamin's place and argued: My father pleaded with us not to take Binyamin down to Egypt. Now "how can I go up to my father if the youth is not with me?[10] When he sees that the youth is missing, he will die!"[11]

Yoseph's response was: "I am Yoseph. Is my father still alive?" — If you are worried that Father will die of grief because Binyamin is missing, why didn't you worry about Father's grief when you sold me?[12]

---

9. *Bereshit Rabbah.*
10. Bereshit 44:34.
11. Bereshit 44:31.
12. See *Bet HaLevi.*

But why was this a rebuke? Yehudah had already addressed this question! He had said that Binyamin comforted Yaakov for Rachel and Yoseph who he had lost and if anything happened to Binyamin, Yaakov would feel as if all three had died the same day.[13] Whereas when Yoseph disappeared, Yaakov still had Binyamin.

We may explain that since Yoseph was especially beloved to Yaakov, Yehudah should have worried that Yaakov might have also died of grief when Yoseph disappeared.

Yet the *Bet HaLevi's* interpretation is still puzzling. There are two reasons why Yehudah said he was worried about Yaakov's grief concerning Binyamin but he was not worried about Yaakov's grief when they sold Yosef. Firstly, Yehudah did not say to Yosef that he was worried about Yaakov, rather he reported that Yaakov himself had said that he would die if Binyamin would not return. Secondly, when they sold Yosef they were carrying out the *bet din's* verdict and thus Yehudah didn't concern himself with Yaakov's feelings. But Binyamin was a different matter.

The *Bet HaLevi* may be understood as follows.

The brothers were absolutely sure that they were right; they had irrefutable arguments for selling Yoseph. Then they heard, "I am Yoseph. Is my father still alive?" Suddenly all their arguments melted away, and the truth became exposed. The underlying reason for the sale was bad *midot*. Their jealousy and hatred caused them not to be concerned with Yaakov's grief. Had they considered Yaakov's grief they would have arrived at the correct conclusion — that Yoseph was innocent.

Herein lies a lesson for all of us.

We are confident that we are right; we have irrefutable arguments for whatever we do. But one day we will face Hashem — and

---

13. See Bereshit 44:27–29, Rashi.

suddenly all our arguments will melt away, exposing the truth: that the real reason for our actions was bad *midot*.

The Midrash continues:

> Rabbi Elazar ben Azaryah [wept[14] and] said: Woe to us from the Day of Judgment! Woe to us from the Day of Rebuke!
>
> When Yoseph HaTzaddik, who was flesh and blood, rebuked his brothers, they could not stand before his rebuke. When Hashem, Who is the Judge and the Litigant, [rebukes us], how much more so!

What does Rabbi Elazar ben Azaryah add to what the Midrash already said?

We may find the answer in the second part of Yoseph's rebuke: "I am your brother Yoseph, whom you sold into Egypt."[15]

A question was hanging in the air, even if it wasn't asked: Why had Yoseph treated his brothers as he had? Why had he falsely accused them of espionage, and planted the money and later the goblet in their satchels? Why had he arrested Shimon, forced them to bring Binyamin, invited them all to dinner, and afterwards threatened to take Binyamin as a slave?

Yoseph answered, "I did all these strange things so that you would examine your deeds, as a person should do when afflictions come upon him.

"I gave you hints so that you yourselves would understand that I am Yoseph and that all of my dreams were prophetic — not, as you thought, that I dreamt at night about what had been on my mind during the day.

"I accused you falsely to make you realize that you had accused me falsely when you sold me.

"When you entered Egypt separately, through many gates, I

---

14. *Hagigah* 4b.
15. *Bereshit* 45:4.

could have judged you favorably; perhaps there was an innocent explanation. Instead, I accused you of espionage. This was to make you realize that you hadn't judged me favorably; perhaps I was trying to help you ascend to a higher level in kashrut, unity, and holiness. Instead, you decided that I was a *rodef* who wanted to cut you off from the Jewish people."

That is why Rabbi Elazar ben Azaryah wept. He learned from here that one day, each of us will stand judgment before Hashem in the world to come, and Hashem will judge us exactly as we judged others. If we gave others the benefit of the doubt, Hashem will give us the benefit of the doubt, too. But if we judged others negatively, "Woe to us from the Day of Judgment! Woe to us from the Day of Rebuke!"

BELIEVE IT OR NOT

Then Yoseph said to his brothers, "Come close to me, please," and they came close. And he said, "I am your brother Yoseph, whom you sold into Egypt." (Bereshit 45:4)

"Behold, your eyes see, as do the eyes of my brother Binyamin, that it is my mouth that is speaking to you [in your language[16]]." (Bereshit 45:12)

Even after all the hints and finally the declaration "I am Yoseph," the brothers could not believe that the viceroy was Yoseph. Finally, he convinced them of his identity with two proofs, hinted in these two verses; that he was circumcised, and that he spoke the Hebrew language.

Why didn't the brothers believe he was Yoseph?

---

16. Targum.

We believe what our eyes see; to us, that is reality. Should it contradict a teaching of our Sages, we devise convoluted interpretations to align the teaching with it. But to the brothers, reality was Torah.

Thus the Gemara[17] relates that Rabbi Yohanan said, "Yaakov Avinu did not die." An objection was raised, "Did they lament him for nothing?" Rabbi Yohanan retorted, "I am expounding a verse," and he proceeded to do so.

Says Rashi: "They lamented Yaakov because *they thought* he had died." Rabbi Shalom Shwadron[18] explained that to Rabbi Yohanan, reality was the verse; if we see lamenting, it is because *they thought* he had died.

Yoseph had been convicted as a *rodef* in a *din Torah*.[19] To the brothers, the verdict of a *din Torah* is reality. So even after he told them, "I am Yoseph," they did not believe it, and he had to prove it to them with his circumcision and with the Holy Tongue.

What kind of proof was circumcision? After all, the entire Egyptian populace was circumcised because Yoseph had made them undergo circumcision before he would give them food!

And, as the Ramban asks, what kind of proof was speaking Hebrew? All of Canaan spoke Hebrew, and many kings speak the languages of neighboring lands!

An answer to the Ramban's question may be found in the Targum: "It is my mouth that is speaking to you in your language." The proof was not the Hebrew itself, but Yoseph's manner of speaking, which was typical of Yaakov's house. He said, "It was for

---

17. *Taanit* 5b.
18. Citing his teacher.
19. Litigation according to Torah.

sustenance that God sent me ahead of you,"[20] and "God sent me ahead of you"[21] — it isn't your fault, it's Hashem's plan. "God has made me master of all Egypt"[22] — it isn't my talent; it's Hashem's design.

Yoseph spoke the language of faith in Hashem, gracious reconciliation, and Torah. This is the language of Yaakov's house. Similarly, when Yoseph told the brothers to ask Yaakov to come to Egypt "lest you become impoverished,"[23] he meant spiritual poverty, as the *Baal HaTurim* says; the famine was liable to make the house of Yaakov poor in Torah.

The only way Yoseph could convince the brothers that they erred in their *din Torah* was through faith, Torah — and holiness.

The covenant of circumcision is more than a one-time surgical procedure; it's a lifetime commitment to holiness. When this holiness is safeguarded, it has the power to frighten off a lion. Yoseph showed the brothers his holiness.

Proof that to the brothers, reality was Torah, comes from Yoseph's admonition, *Al tirgizu badarech,* "Do not become agitated on the way,"[24] which Rashi explains to mean that Yoseph warned them against becoming deeply immersed in Torah study lest they lose their way, as can happen to great Torah scholars.

Despite their intense devotion to Torah, the brothers had erred in their *din Torah* because "his brothers were jealous of him."[25] Flawed *midot* can ruin anyone's judgment.

---

20. Bereshit 45:5.
21. Bereshit 45:7.
22. Bereshit 45:9.
23. Bereshit 45:11.
24. Bereshit 45:24.
25. Bereshit 37:11.

WEEPING IN ADVANCE

After Yosef revealed himself to his brothers *He fell upon the neck of his brother Binyamin and wept, and Binyamin wept upon his neck.* (Bereshit 45:14)

Rashi writes that Yoseph wept over the two Temples in Jerusalem, which were in in Binyamin's territory, and Binyamin wept over the Tabernacle in Shilo, which was in Yoseph's territory, both of which would eventually be destroyed.

Why did they weep now over the destruction of Sanctuaries that hadn't yet been built? If a prophet would tell us today, "A thousand years from now, a great tzaddik will be born; and at the age of eighty he will die and all will mourn," would we weep now?

We may answer in light of the Midrash on the verse, "Yoseph dreamed a dream, which he told his brothers.... He said to them, 'Hear, now, this dream that I dreamt.'"[26] The Midrash[27] expounds that he said to them that the prophets will rebuke you using the same language, "Hear, now, the word of Hashem."

From here we learn that Yoseph had been speaking as a prophet when he rebuked them about their kashrut, unity, and morality. Later, when they came down to Egypt to buy food, Yoseph again tried to make them realize their error and accept his prophecy willingly. Why was this so important to Yoseph?

The deeds of the fathers of our people foreshadowed what would befall their offspring (*maaseh avot siman lebanim*). The brothers threw Yoseph into a pit for rebuking them, and the Jewish people did the same to the prophet Yirmiyahu a thousand years later.[28] Had the brothers accepted Yoseph's prophetic re-

---

26. Bereshit 37:5–6.
27. *Bereshit Rabbah* 4:10.
28. See *Bereshit Rabbah* 93:12; Yirmiyahu, ch. 31.

buke, the Jewish people would have accepted Yirmiyahu's — and the First Temple would not have been destroyed. Now Yoseph wept over his failure to prevent its destruction. He also wept over his failure to stop the dissension among Yaakov's sons, which foreshadowed the *sinat hinam*[29] among the Jewish people that destroyed the Second Temple.

Binyamin wept over the lack of leadership among the brothers when Yoseph was separated from the family. The same lack of leadership among the Jewish people — when Eli the Kohen Gadol grew old and his sons did not follow in his ways — caused the destruction of the Tabernacle in Shilo.

WHAT KIND OF HOUSE?

[Yaakov] sent Yehudah ahead of him to Yoseph, to prepare (lehorot) ahead of him in Goshen. (Bereshit 46:28)

What was Yehudah sent ahead to prepare?

The Midrash[30] offers two answers: a home to live in, or a house of study in which Torah would be taught and studied.

A house of study is alluded to in the word *lehorot*, which literally means "to teach." But where do we find a hint of a home? Besides, it's obvious that a home had to be prepared. Why do we need a verse to tell us this?

Evidently, a home is not just a place for eating and sleeping, but also for teaching and instructing. A home is where parents transmit instruction to future generations. And in contrast to a house of study, where *horaah*[31] is given only when the Rav is asked

29. Baseless hatred.
30. *Bereshit Rabbah* 95:3.
31. Halachic ruling.

a question, at home *horaah* is given freely by the parents. (Thus when calling a married man up to the Torah, we say, *"Yaamod haRav..."*[32]).

The *horaah* at home is given mainly by example. If the father is particular to *daven*[33] with a *minyan*[34] and not to speak *lashon hara*,[35] he is giving positive instruction. But if he gets angry, he is giving negative instruction.

Both opinions in the Midrash are true — Yehudah prepared both a home and a house of study. Both are reflected in the continuation of the Midrash

> This teaches that wherever Yaakov dwelt, he studied Torah, just as Avraham and Yitzhak had done.
>
> How did Avraham Avinu know the Torah?
>
> One opinion is that his two kidneys became like pitchers of water, and Torah flowed from them. Another opinion is that he learned it from himself [that is, from the Divine inspiration within him]. Avraham knew even [the Rabbinical ordinance of] *eruvei tavshilin*.

The two opinions in the Midrash may be understood as follows. Next to the kidneys are the adrenal glands, which send adrenaline flowing into the bloodstream when we need extra energy for a fight. Our biggest fight is against our worst enemy, the evil inclination. We need tremendous energy and might to control our temper or overcome laziness, lust, stinginess, and selfishness. Accordingly, the Midrash is saying that education to good *midot* flowed from Avraham's kidneys, and knowledge of Torah and mitzvot from his Divine inspiration.

---

32. Let the Rav stand.
33. Pray.
34. Quorum of ten men.
35. "The evil tongue" — speaking negatively about others.

The Midrash aptly concludes with Hashem's statement: "I love [Avraham] because he will command his children and his household after him to keep the way of Hashem, doing charity and justice."[36] The Rambam[37] explains that Hashem loved Avraham for educating his family to good *midot*, for instance, by encouraging compassion and strengthening humility.

The Mussar authorities compare the home to a yeshiva, which has a Rosh Yeshiva and Mashgiah. In the home, the father serves as Rosh Yeshiva, learning Torah with the children and the mother serves as Mashgiah, "supervising the ways of her household,"[38] educating the children to *derech eretz,*[39] good *midot*, and fear of heaven.

If we build our homes on this model, we will draw down Hashem's love as Avraham did.

---

36. Bereshit 18:19.
37. *Hilchot De'ot,* end of ch. 1.
38. Mishlei 31:27.
39. Proper, refined behavior.

PARASHAT

Vayehi

THE END OF DAYS

Yaakov called for his sons and said, "Assemble and I will tell you what will befall you in the End of Days."(Bereshit 49:1)

Rashi comments:

Yaakov sought to reveal the End (קץ). But the Shechinah departed from him, and he began to say other things.

Daat Zekenim adds:

Yaakov wondered why his sons were unworthy of having the End revealed to them. After all, there was no sin in them, as evident by the fact that the letters ח and ט of חטא, "sin," do not appear in their names.

Divine inspiration replied, "But neither do ק and ץ, so they are unworthy of knowing the קץ, "End."

Why was the date of Mashiah's coming withheld from Yaakov's sons? Let's try to understand the *Daat Zekenim*'s explanation.

If a person knew the date of his death, he might sin for years and count on repairing the harm by repenting before death. Similarly, if we knew the date of Mashiah's coming, perhaps only the generation immediately before would strive to make themselves worthy of it.

Yaakov thought that since his sons were without sin, knowing the End would not hurt them. They, in turn, could transmit it only to the righteous among their descendants.

But he was told that there is another reason for concealing the End: to bring tremendous merit to the Jewish people, who await the redemption. Similarly, Hashem increased Avraham's merit by concealing the exact destination when He told Avraham to go "to the land that I will show you,"[1] and bind Yitzhak "on one of the mountains that I will tell you."[2]

Centuries of awaiting the redemption have brought the Jewish people unimaginable merit. The mitzvah of looking forward to Mashiah's coming is recorded in the Rambam:[3]

> The Messianic king is destined to arise and restore the kingship of David.... And whoever does not believe in him *or await his coming...* is denying the Torah and Moshe Rabbenu....

How should we await his coming? Says the Hafetz Hayyim: Picture a beloved uncle living far away who has sent his family a letter saying, "One day, I'll come for a visit." Whenever there is a knock at the door, everyone in the house jumps for joy, thinking "Maybe Uncle has come!"

But if knowledge of the date had to be concealed for our benefit, why did Yaakov say, "I will tell you what will befall you in the End of Days"? No unfulfilled word ever issued from Yaakov's mouth![4] How could a "wasted" statement have come from Yaakov? And why should the Torah record it?

To find the answer, let's investigate another question on the

1. Bereshit 12:1.
2. Bereshit 22:2
3. *Hilchot Melachim* 11:1.
4. *Bet HaShoevah,* citing Midrash.

verse. It actually says יקרא, "will call." But Targum translates as if it said יקרה, "will befall." How can we reconcile the two?

When one wants to acquire an animal, the halacha is that it becomes his by drawing it to him. It can be drawn either by calling the animal or by hitting it with a stick. In Shir HaShirim,[5] the Jewish people say to Hashem, "Draw me; we will run after You." We ask Hashem to acquire us as His possession, but we pray that Hashem not draw us by hitting us, rather by calling to us so that we will come running after Him.

In our times, many Jews hear Hashem's call and return to Him. To one, a grandfather came in a dream; a second awakened by himself; a third attended a Judaism seminar. The stories of what led to repentance are endless — and all are examples of calls that people heard.

Accordingly, Yaakov told his sons: What will befall (יקרה) you in the End of Days is that Hashem will call (יקרא) out to the Jewish people and they will return to Him.

Our era is the End of Days, and we are seeing this happen before our very eyes. So although Yaakov was not allowed to give the date of the redemption, he did describe it, and his words have been fulfilled.

Some seventy years ago, Rabbi Shelomo of Zevil said, "Soon, you will meet people in the street who look like grandchildren of the Baal Shem Tov but who, only a year before, were big sinners."

"Rebbe," asked his followers, "how do you know?"

Rabbi Shelomo replied, "At the end of the night, the sun sends forth a few rays of light from just beneath the horizon. This is the dim light of dawn, which is soon followed by sunrise. Similarly, at the end of the exile, rays of repentance will begin to shine. This

5. 1:4. Explanation follows *Tuv HaPeninim*.

dim light will soon be followed by the sunrise of Mashiah, when everyone will be aroused to repent."

Our era is the dawn. It will soon be followed by the glorious sunrise. At that time, *uva leTzion goel,* "the redeemer shall come to Zion, and to those of Yaakov who repent from sin."

YAAKOV'S BLESSINGS

This is what their father spoke to them, and he blessed them. He blessed each according to his blessing. (Bereshit 49:28)

How can the verse say that Yaakov blessed all his sons when several of his sons received rebuke not blessings?

The Gemara[6] relates a man was wont to say, *Dunu dini,* "Judge my case!" Investigation revealed that he was from the Tribe of Dan to whom Yaakov had blessed saying, "Dan will judge." Another man was wont to say, "If I were to build a house, I would build it on the seashore." Investigation revealed that he was from the Tribe of Zevulun, whom Yaakov blessed: "Zevulun will settle by the seashore."[7]

These anecdotes took place in Babylon in the time of the Gemara and we can learn from here that the Ten Tribes were not totally lost and members of the Ten Tribes exist among the Jewish people today.

We also learn that a person's characteristics are inherited by his offspring for many generations to come. Accordingly, we may say that Yaakov's "blessed" his sons by revealing their characteristics, so that they could use them as tools for success.

Thus when Yaakov told Reuven that he acted rashly, he was telling him: You have the good trait of seeing the suffering of

---

6. *Pesahim* 4a.
7. Bereshit 49:13.

others. You saw Yoseph's suffering and took action to save him. You also saw your mother's suffering, and took action on her behalf by rearranging the beds — but here you acted rashly, for what you did was disrespectful to your father. You need to know when to use your good trait.

Yaakov told Shimon and Levi that they didn't control their anger. Shimon's trait was to listen and be aroused by what he heard. Levi's was to join the zealous. Both avenged the honor of a Jewish girl. The problem was that they didn't consult their father before doing it.

The Levites in Moshe's time inherited the trait of zealotry for Hashem's honor. Moshe said, "Whoever is for Hashem, to me!"[8] — and the Levites immediately joined Moshe in zealotry. The Shimonites did not. They remembered their father's warning to be extremely cautious before going out to kill.

In light of this, we can understand Yaakov's introductory words, "Gather together and listen, O sons of Yaakov, and listen to your father, Yisrael."[9] Targum renders: Listen, sons of Yaakov, and accept instruction from your father, Yisrael.

What is the "instruction"? Yaakov was about to bless them, not teach them!

Evidently the essence of the blessing was that Yaakov Avinu prophetically taught each one his unique characteristic. Today, in the absence of a prophet, people often make mistakes in this area. Instead of developing their potential by putting their God-given talents to good use, they go into occupations for which they are unsuited. The result is lack of success and fulfillment in their chosen occupation as well as a waste of their unused talents.

---

8. Shemot 32:26.
9. Bereshit 49:2.

It is told that a youth once went to consult his Mashgiah, who took him to the window from which they could see the market-place.

"What do you see?" the Mashgiah asked him.

"I see one man selling potatoes, a second selling carrots, a third selling oranges...."

"No," said the Mashgiah. "You see a cemetery. On the forehead of the first, it says, 'Here a Rosh Yeshiva is buried.' On the forehead of the second, it says, 'Here a Mashgiah is buried.' On the forehead of the third, it says, 'Here a great Rav is buried.'"

The real blessing is to develop our own unique characteristics and put them to good use.

Humash
Shemot

PARASHAT

Shemot

LIKE THE STARS

And these are the names of the sons of Yisrael who were coming to Egypt; with Yaakov, each man and his household came. (Shemot 1:1)

The Torah already said this in Parashat Vayigash.[1] Why repeat it here?

Rashi writes:

Although He listed them by name during their lifetime, He listed them again after their death, to make known that they were cherished. They were likened to the stars, which He takes out and brings in by number and by name, as it is written, "He brings forth their hosts by number; He calls to each of them by name."[2]

How does this answer the question?

And why does the Torah here repeat that "Yoseph died, and all his brothers...,[3] when Yoseph's death was already mentioned at the end of Humash Bereshit?

Finally, immediately afterwards the Torah states:

---

1. Bereshit 46:8.
2. Yeshayahu 40:26.
3. Shemot 1:6.

Benei Yisrael were fruitful, teemed, increased, and became extremely strong, and the land became filled with them.[4]

Why does this follow the mentioning of the names of the Shevatim?

All of these questions can be answered in light of the Midrash:[5]

The Shevatim are mentioned here because they all allude to the redemption of Israel:[6] Reuven [whose name means "see"] — for "I have seen the affliction of My people."[7] Shimon [whose name means "hear"] — for "God heard their groaning." [8]Levi [whose name means "join'] — for Hashem joined them in the suffering, as it is written, "I am with him in distress."[9] Yehudah [whose name means "thank'] — for they thanked Hashem....

Each Shevet was named for a particular *midah* that he would be raised to specialize in (see Parashat Vayetzei). Thus Reuven and Shimon saw and heard people in distress, Levi knew whom to join, and Yehudah was a master of gratitude. The Shevatim raised their own children to specialize in these same traits. The Torah records their names after the Shevatim left this world to tell us that their *midot* still exist here; and in the merit of these names — *midot,* their descendants would be redeemed from Egypt.

The Midrash[10] continues:

"Yoseph died, and all his brothers...." — to teach that as long as one of those who went down to Egypt was alive, the Egyptians did not subjugate Israel.

---

4. Shemot 1:7.
5. *Bereshit Rabbah* 1:5.
6. See our discussion in Parashat Vayetzei.
7. Shemot 3:7.
8. Shemot 2:24.
9. Tehilim 91:15.
10. *Bereshit Rabbah* 1:8.

"Benei Yisrael were fruitful, teemed..." — although Yoseph and his brothers had died, their God lives forever.

What is the Midrash telling us?

Hashem is like the king who takes the children of his deceased friend under his wing giving them better care than they had while their father was alive. In the merit of the Shevatim, whom He loved, Hashem took their descendants under His wing showering them with blessing, so that their population increased miraculously, more than while the Shevatim were alive.

Similarly, we sometimes see that when a Rosh Yeshiva dies, Hashem takes the yeshiva under His wing, so that it flourishes even more than while the Rosh Yeshiva was alive.

Now we can understand Rashi's comparison of the Shevatim to stars. "Good are the luminaries that our God created.... He granted them power and might to rule the world."[11] Just as in the daytime, when the stars are not seen, they continue to affect the world, so too, even when the Shevatim, are no longer with us, the good *midot* they inculcated in future generations continue to exist here, bringing blessing and redemption to their descendants.

THE MIDWIVES STAND UP TO PHARAOH

The midwives feared God, and they did not do as the king of Egypt spoke to them. And they caused the boys to live. (Shemot 1:17)

The midwives did two things, as the Gemara[12] explains. Besides disobeying Pharaoh's orders to kill the baby boys, they also "caused the boys to live" by providing them with food and water. Rashi adds, that the midwives took the babies into their own

---

11. Shaharit of Shabbat.
12. *Sotah* 11b.

homes. The Torah records Pharaoh's reaction and the midwives' response:

> The king of Egypt summoned the midwives and said to them, "Why did you do this thing, causing the boys to live?"

> The midwives said to Pharaoh, "Because the Hebrew women are not like the Egyptian women; they are experts. Even before the midwife comes to them, they have given birth."[13]

How did the midwives dare give Pharaoh such a ridiculous answer? The very fact that they were midwives proved that the Hebrew women needed help giving birth! Besides, the answer doesn't address Pharaoh's question, which was why they "caused the boys to live" by providing them with food and water.

The question is intensified when contrasted with an anecdote from Czarist Russia.[14] After the Russian railroad was completed, Czar Nicholai summoned the engineer in charge of the project in order to thank him. The engineer came and stood before Nicholai — and turned speechless from fright.

When the midwives stood before Pharaoh, they did not turn speechless. On the contrary, they ignored Pharaoh's question, gave an "answer" that made a mockery of him, and even insulted the Egyptian women by saying that the Jewish women were stronger and better! How could the midwives be so fearless?

Hovot HaLevavot[15] teaches that to a pious person, fear of Hashem banishes all other fears. If a person is standing before an uncaged lion, and just then a bee buzzes near him, does he feel any fear of the bee? "The midwives feared God," and this fear banished

---

13. Shemot 1:18–19.
14. Related by Rabbi Eliyahu Lopian.
15. *Shaar Heshbon HaNefesh,* ch. 3.

any fear of Pharaoh, for after all, who was Pharaoh in comparison to the Creator?

Interestingly, Pharaoh did not punish the midwives; he simply let them go. This is typical of gentiles. Often when they see that a Jew is strong in his faith, they let him be.

From the midwives we see that a Jew has the ability to totally subjugate his emotions and his limbs to Hashem's command. A more recent example comes from the Rav of Tchebin. It is told that when this great *gaon* was old, he needed to undergo a medical procedure that required him to be wide awake. The doctors were afraid he might doze in the middle. He assured them that he would stay awake. How? He would lay tefillin. Since the Halachah forbids sleeping with tefillin on, he would definitely not fall asleep.

Such high levels come from *devekut,* cleaving to Hashem, which the Ramban[16] explains as:

> ...remembering and loving Him always, such that his thoughts never leave Him even when going on the way, lying down, or waking up, to the point that his words with men are with his mouth and tongue, but his heart is not with them; it is before Hashem.
>
> ...when people are on this level, their souls are bound in the bonds of life even during their lifetime, for they themselves are a dwelling place for the Shechinah.

In his heart, such a person is always walking with Hashem, as the prophet Michah enjoined us to do when he said, "What does Hashem require of you but to do justice, love kindness, and walk humbly with your God?"[17]

A person who lives this way will fear Hashem alone, as the

---

16. Devarim 11:22.
17. Michah 6:8.

midwives did, to the point where all other fears and worries vanish. This is the level to which we should aspire.

NOW I KNOW WHY

After Moshe killed an Egyptian he saw two Jewish men fighting. When he reprimanded one of them, he told Moshe, *"Who appointed you as a dignitary, ruler, and judge over us? Do you propose to kill me as you killed the Egyptian?"*

Moshe was frightened, and he thought, "Indeed, the matter is known!" (Shemot 2:14)

Rashi, citing the Midrash, explains what Moshe was thinking: "I always wondered, what sin did the Jewish people do, that caused them to be subjugated more harshly than the seventy nations. Now I see why they deserve it."

Egypt was filled with male and female slaves from other lands as we see that in the tenth plague, Hashem smote "from the firstborn of Pharaoh... to the firstborn of the maidservant."[18] During the great famine, their ancestors had come to Egypt to buy grain, and when they ran out of money, Yoseph acquired them as slaves for Pharaoh in exchange for the grain. Moshe wondered why these slaves were not treated as harshly as the Jews.

Now he knew that the harsh treatment of the Jews was due to *lashon hara*, for he saw that they were talking about his killing of the Egyptian and might even report it to Pharaoh.[19]

But this contradicts the Midrash:

In the merit of five things our forefathers were redeemed from Egypt: They did not change their names, garments, or language;

---

18. Shemot 11:5.
19. See Rashi 2:14.

nor did they speak *lashon hara,* or sully themselves with immorality.[20]

Were the Jews subjugated because they spoke *lashon hara,* or were they redeemed for not speaking it?

We may explain as follows.

The Jews surely separated themselves from the Egyptians in these five ways. Had they assumed Egyptian names, dress, and language, and certainly had they married Egyptians, the Jews would have assimilated. And had they informed on their fellow Jews, they would have curried favor with the Egyptians and become closer to them. But this does not mean that the Jews wanted to leave Egypt. In fact, at times, after they left and were journeying through the desert, they expressed a wish to return.

The Jews had a tradition that one day a redeemer would take them out of Egypt. Now young Moshe came along and shared their burden, lent them a helping hand, and even killed an Egyptian taskmaster who was beating a Jewish slave. In Moshe, they saw the beginnings of a redeemer — but since they didn't want to leave they spoke *lashon hara* against him.

Moshe said, "Now I understand that the reason the Jews are oppressed more than others is so that they should desire redemption! The others, who are not destined for redemption, are subjugated in a normal manner. Jews are subjugated excessively because they are destined for redemption."

This principle applies throughout history. To this very day, if we suffer more than other nations, it is to make us desire the redemption for which we are destined.

---

20. *Vayikra Rabbah* 35.

THE BURNING BUSH

*An angel of Hashem appeared to him in a flame of fire from amid the
thorn bush. He saw, and behold, the thorn bush was burning in the
fire, but the thorn bush was not consumed.*

*Moshe thought, "I will turn aside now and look at this great sight.
Why isn't the thorn bush burnt?"*

*Hashem saw that he turned aside to look, and God called out to
him from amid the thorn bush...* (Shemot 3:2–4)

The Midrash [21] comments:

Rabbi Yohanan said: At that moment, Moshe took five steps, as
it is written, אסורה, I will turn aside now and look." [It says אסורה
instead of אסור. The extra *hey* has a numerical value of five.]

Rabbi Shimon ben Lakish said: He turned his head and looked,
as it is written, "Hashem saw that he turned aside to look."
Hashem looked at him and said, "This one is fitting to tend Benei
Yisrael."

Rabbi Yitzhak said: What is meant by *ki sar lirot*, "he turned
aside to look"? He was distressed (*sar veza'ef*) to see the pain of
the Jewish people in Egypt. Therefore he was worthy of being their
shepherd. Immediately, "God called out to him...."

Why should taking five steps or turning his head make Moshe
worthy of becoming Israel's leader?

All the narratives about Moshe involve the quality of *nosei be'ol*;
Moshe always "shared the yoke" with his bretheren. The Torah
relates that he saved a Jew from the Egyptian who was beating
him and then intervened when one Jew was hitting another. The
Midrash adds that he wept for his people and said, "Would that I
would die instead of them." Afterwards, he rescued Yitro's daughters
from the shepherds even though they were not his people.

---

21. Shemot Rabbah 6.

All this took place when Moshe witnessed injustice. Now, he was in the desert, far from his fellow Jews, yet when he saw only a hint of their suffering through the burning thorn bush,[22] he was immediately reminded of his brothers' pain and his compassion made him ask, "Why isn't the thorn bush burned?" — Why aren't the enemies of the Jews destroyed?

In his overriding concern for them, Moshe took five steps forward as if to rescue his people, turned his head to think how to do it, and even felt distress over their pain.

The slight hint elicited these three responses because the trait of *nosei be'ol* was so deeply ingrained in Moshe that even from afar, his thoughts were always on his suffering brothers.

We can apply this concept to the mitzvah of tzitzit, of which the Torah says, "You shall see it, and you shall remember all Hashem's mitzvot, and you shall do them."[23] How do we remember all 613 mitzvot by seeing tzitzit?

Rashi explains: The numerical value of the Hebrew word ציצית equals 600 if we add 8 for the number of threads and 5 for the number of knots it equals 613. Our Sages added: The color of *techelet* resembles the sea, the sea resembles the sky, and the sky resembles the heavenly throne.

How do these far-fetched hints cause us to remember all the mitzvot and prepare ourselves to fulfill them?

If we develop a desire to fulfill all Hashem's mitzvot as strong as Moshe's trait of *nosei be'ol,* tzitzit will remind us of the mitzvot, just as the Burning Bush reminded Moshe of his brothers' suffering.

---

22. Michael, the heavenly prince of Israel, was in the burning thorn bush to symbolize the Jewish people suffering at the hands of its enemies. Hashem then told Moshe, "I know its pains."
23. Bamidbar 15:39.

HASHEM'S NAMES

Moshe said to God, "...behold, when... they say to me, 'What is His Name?', what shall I say to them?"

Hashem answered Moshe, "I Shall Be As I Shall Be." And He said, "So shall you say to Benei Yisrael, 'I Shall Be, has sent me to you.'"
(Shemot 3:13 –14)

Rashi explains why Hashem originally said, *I Shall Be As I Shall Be,* and at the end said, *I Shall Be, has sent me*:

Hashem said, "I shall be with them in this exile, and I shall be with them in other exiles."

Moshe said, "Why should I mention future troubles? Isn't a trouble in its own time enough?"

Hashem said, "Go tell them, 'I Shall Be, has sent me to you.'"

But how could Moshe give Hashem advice? Who knows better than He?

We may explain as follows. Moshe thought he was to deliver a prophecy about another exile from which Hashem would redeem them. So he said, "Since my mission now is to encourage the people, let me deliver this prophecy at some other time. Otherwise, I will be lowering their spirits when I am supposed to be raising them."

Hashem explained, "You misunderstood My intention. I want the Jewish people to know how powerful the redemption from Egypt will be — enough to generate all future redemptions."

In fact, it is with us to this day. That's why Shabbat, holidays, tefillin, mezuzah, and many more of our mitzvot are *zecher litziat mitzrayim,* "in remembrance of the departure from Egypt."

What a joyous message! It conveys that we became Hashem's beloved people, whom He would redeem always, under any conditions. Even if we fall a little, we will always be able to get up again.

THEY WON'T BELIEVE ME

And G-d also said ... They will heed your voice. Moshe replied[24] and said, "But behold, they will not believe me and will not heed my voice, for they will say, 'Hashem did not appear to you!'" (Shemot 4:1)

How could Moshe say that Benei Yisrael would not believe him? Hashem had just told him, "They will heed your voice"![25]

We may explain that Moshe was praising the Jewish people, saying: Gentiles believe anyone who claims to be a prophet, receive a book from God, or see an angel — even without witnesses to confirm his claim. Jews, to their credit, are skeptical and don't believe such claims.

Moshe was saying: How can I fulfill your command, for they are sure to ask me, "How do we know that Hashem appeared to you?"

In response Hashem gave Moshe three signs, which would explain to the Jews how it was possible to overcome their three great concerns. Namely, that, Egypt was a mighty empire; secondly, they were subjugated under Pharaoh, who was feared by the kings of all other nations; and thirdly, the Egyptians controlled all the powers of sorcery.

First, Hashem gave him the sign of the staff that turned into a serpent and then back into a staff. The serpent symbolized the mighty Egyptian empire that cast fear over the whole world. But this empire was built by Hashem and given only temporary powers, eventually it will disappear from the scene as if it had never been. Indeed, throughout history, many mighty empires have risen only to fall into oblivion.

Then, after Moshe put his hand to his heart, Hashem struck

---

24. Translation follows Targum.
25. Shemot 3:18.

his hand with leprosy. This sign hinted that "I will send all My plagues to your [Pharaoh's] heart... so that you shall know that there is none like Me in all the earth."[26] The Ten Plagues striking Pharaoh's person and his wealth would bring him to his knees.

Finally, Hashem told Moshe to take water from the Nile and turn it into blood. The Nile, worshiped by the Egyptians, symbolized their idolatry and sorcery. Hashem was hinting that just as the Nile would turn putrid and revolting, all the powers of idolatry and sorcery would crumble.[27]

If indeed Moshe based his question on the virtue of the Jewish people, who do not believe unfounded claims, why does Rashi, commenting on the verse "But behold, they will not believe me", say, that Moshe spoke ill of them? Wasn't their skepticism a virtue?

The Hafetz Hayyim answers that the problem was only with the word *Behold*, which conveys certainty. Moshe should have said, "Perhaps."

Thus the Midrash[28] says: When Hashem said to Moshe, "*Behold*, your days have approached to die,"[29] Moshe said, "I praised you with *Behold*, saying, ['*Behold* to Hashem, your God, are the heavens... '30] — and with *Behold*, You decree death on me?!"

Hashem replied, "Don't you remember that when I sent you to redeem the Jews from Egypt, you said, '*Behold* they will not believe me'?"

Thus the complaint against Moshe was only about the word *Behold*.

---

26. Shemot 9:14.
27. See Shemot 12:12, Rashi.
28. *Devarim Rabbah* 9:6.
29. Devarim 31:14.
30. Devarim 10:14.

Va'era

WHAT WENT WRONG?

*God spoke to Moshe and said to him, "I am Hashem. I appeared to
Avraham, to Yitzhak, and to Yaakov as E-l Shad-dai, but with My
Name Hashem I did not make Myself known to them."* (Shemot 6:2–3)

Why did Hashem start speaking to Moshe about His Names,
and why did He mention each of the Forefathers?

To answer these questions, let's go back to the end of the previous Parashah, where Moshe and Aharon first asked Pharaoh to let
Benei Yisrael go. In reaction, Pharaoh increased their workload
until it was unbearable; besides meeting the usual quota of bricks,
they would have to supply the straw themselves.

To make matters worse, Pharaoh took away their day of rest.
When Moshe was growing up in the palace, he had asked Pharaoh
to give them off on Shabbat. On that day, they would delight in their
books. Perhaps these were the books that Avraham Avinu had written about *emunah*,[1] or perhaps their books spoke of the longed-for
redemption, as our Midrashim speak of the Messianic era. Pharaoh
put an end to this, saying, "Let them not heed false words."[2]

---

1. See Rambam, *Hilchot Avodah Zarah*, ch. 1.
2. Shemot 5:10; *Shemot Rabbah* 5:18.

Worse still, when Moshe left Pharaoh, there were Jews that said to him, "You have made our scent abhorrent in the eyes of Pharaoh and... his servants, to place a sword in their hand to kill us!"[3]

Finally, Aharon, a long-established prophet, who knew through prophecy that six months would pass before they went to Pharaoh again, advised Moshe to send his family back to Midian, telling him, "We're distressed over the Jews who are already here, and you want to bring in more?"

Then Moshe said to Hashem,"My Lord, why have You done evil to this people? Why did You send me? From the time I came to Pharaoh to speak in Your Name, he did evil to this people, and You did not rescue Your people." [4]

In light of this we can understand our verse. Hashem told Moshe, "I appeared to Avraham, to Yitzhak, and to Yaakov as E-l Shad-dai." The Name Shad-dai is an acronym of *she'amar dai,* "He Who said, 'Enough!'" It conveys: He Who said to His world, "Enough!" shall say to our suffering, "Enough!" Hashem had appeared to the Forefathers with this Name to tell them that eventually their suffering would end.

Although the Forefathers underwent suffering they did not complain about how Hashem runs the world.[5] God promised them the Land of Israel — yet Avraham had to pay a fortune for a burial plot when Sara died; the Plishtim quarreled with Yitzhak over wells that he dug;[6] and Yaakov had to buy a lot on which to pitch his tents.[7] In spite of this, they believed that the time would

---

3. Shemot 5:21.
4. Shemot 5:22.
5. See Rashi, Shemot 6:9.
6. See Bereshit, ch. 26.
7. See Bereshit 33:19.

come when the Land of Israel would be given to their descendants as an inheritance.

Hashem continued, "But with My Name Hashem (YKVK — "He was, is, and will be") I did not make Myself known to them." The Hafetz Hayyim explains with a parable.

A visitor staying in town for Shabbat, noticed that the *gabbai* gave the first *aliyah* to a congregant sitting on the left side, the second to one sitting on the right, and the third to one sitting in the back. The visitor said to the *gabbai,* "I don't understand why you distribute *aliyot* in such a haphazard way. Why don't you start on one side and follow the order of the seats?"

The *gabbai* laughed. "Those who are here all the time understand. The first needed an *aliyah* because he has yartzeit, the second has a new baby, and the third returned from a trip. You're here for one Shabbat, and you want to understand everything?"

Similarly, Hashem said: Only one who was, is, and will be, can understand why things are the way they are. If you see a single piece of a large jigsaw puzzle, you will not understand how it fits in with the whole picture. Although the Forefathers weren't shown the whole picture they believed that ultimately the whole picture would become clear, and it will become known how all the pieces connect.

Upon closer inspection, when Moshe said, "Why have You done evil to this people?" it is not the complaint that it appears to be. Moshe was making three points:

"Why have You done evil to this people?" — This can be interpreted as a prayer, as in "Why do you forget us forever?"[8]

"Why did You send *me*?" — It's must be my fault that the mission failed. I should have let Aharon speak alone, instead I

---

8. Echah 5:20.

joined him, as it says, "They said to Pharaoh."[9] Pharaoh ignored the request because of my speech defect.

"From the *time* I came to Pharaoh..." — If the Jews needed another six months of bondage, I should have been sent to Pharaoh in six months.

Hashem then addressed Moshe's three points.

The suffering must increase for six months because many Jews have grown accustomed to bondage, and tolerating it, they will not want to leave Egypt and go into the desert. If the redemption is not wanted, it won't come. So I must make the suffering unbearable, as the verse says, "I shall take you out from *sivlot mitzrayim*"[10] — which can be interpreted to mean, from tolerating Egypt.

Your mission failed, not because of you, rather, because I made it fail. For after seeing you and Aharon walk past the lions and tigers guarding the entrances to Pharaoh's palace,[11] the Jews began to rely on you to save them. Only after they realized that your help made things worse, did they stop relying on you and turned to Me in prayer.

Similarly, several centuries later, Queen Esther hid her Jewish identity so that the Jews would not say, "We have a sister in the royal palace" and rely on her to save them from Haman's decree. Thus they were frightened into praying wholeheartedly to Hashem, Who then saved them.

Now too, Hashem told Moshe, "I have heard the groaning of Benei Yisrael"[12] — a wholehearted prayer, on account of which I will save them.

The story is told of the man who came running to the doctor.

9. Shemot 5:1.
10. Shemot 6:6.
11. *Yalkut Shimoni.*
12. Bereshit 6:5.

"My father is desperately ill. He can hardly breathe. Come quickly!"

"I first have to put on my tie," said the doctor, and then disappeared into the next room.

After waiting tensely for a few minutes, the man gave up and called out, "Never mind, we'll pray instead."

Immediately the doctor came out and said, "I didn't want you to rely on me to save your father. Now that you are relying on Hashem, I'll do whatever I can."

Hashem was telling Moshe: Your prayer on behalf of Israel, "Why have You done evil to this people?" has been accepted. "Now you will see what I shall do to Pharaoh."[13] Soon the bondage will end.

IN WHAT MERIT?

Hashem said to Moshe and to Aharon... (Shemot 7:8)

In what merit did Hashem redeem Israel? We find three opinions among our Sages.

One opinion is that Hashem, looking for merit among Benei Yisrael to bring the redemption, found nothing but the merit of Moshe and Aharon. The matter may be compared to a king who wished to marry a poor woman who had nothing but two earrings [to bring as dowry], but with these, he married her. Similarly, Hashem redeemed Israel in the merit of Moshe and Aharon, as it is written, "Hashem said to Moshe and to Aharon."[14]

A second opinion is that our ancestors were redeemed from Egypt in the merit of five things: they did not change their names, dress, or language; they did not speak *lashon hara*; and they did not sully themselves with immorality.[15]

---

13. Shemot 6:1.
14. *Shemot Rabbah* 15:3.
15. *Vayikra Rabbah* 32:5.

A third opinion is that the time had come for Hashem to fulfill the promise He had given Avraham to redeem his children, but they lacked mitzvot. So He gave them two mitzvot — the Pesach offering and circumcision, as it says, "Then I passed over you and saw you wallowing in your bloods"[16] — the plural "bloods" is referring to the blood of the Pesach offering and the blood of circumcision.[17]

Was the redemption in the merit of Moshe and Aharon, the five things, or the two mitzvot?

For that matter, why were any merits needed? After all when Hashem promised to give to Avraham the Land of Israel, Avraham asked, "How shall I know that I will inherit it?"[18] Hashem replied, without preconditions, "Your offspring shall be aliens in a land not their own — and they will serve them, and they will oppress them... Afterwards they will leave with great wealth."[19]

An answer may be found in this very statement, which included two decrees: exile, as referred to in, *aliens in a land not their own,* and bondage as referred to in, *and they will serve them, and they will oppress them.* The five things were needed to remove them from exile, and the two mitzvot were needed to extricate them from bondage.

For what purpose did Hashem exile Avraham's offspring in Egypt?

The *Zohar*[20] relates that Rabbi Elazar put this question to his father, Rabbi Shimon bar Yohai, who tossed it back to him. Rabbi Elazar answered: In the Land of Israel, the family of Avraham, Yitzhak, and Yaakov was held in high esteem and well liked. This posed a danger of assimilation and intermarriage. To protect

---

16. Yehezkel 16:6.
17. Rashi on Shemot 12:6, citing Rabbi Matiah ben Harash, who expounds Yehezkel, ch. 16.
18. Bereshit 15:8.
19. Bereshit 15:13–14.
20. Shemot 14b.

them, Hashem sent Yaakov and his family down to the nation of Egypt who disdained the Jews and considered eating with them an abomination; surely they would not intermarry with the Jews.

But on the other hand the Jews were liable to feel inferior, especially after the Egyptians enslaved them and degraded them by giving women's work to men, and making them clean the streets, as the Midrash relates. Hashem weeps over the loss of Jewish pride,[21] for it, too, can lead to assimilation, as it did in the past two centuries.

In Egypt, the Jews withstood this trial with great success. They were proud of their language, dress, and names, and did not embrace Egyptian culture. Nor did they speak ill of their brothers in order to curry favor with their masters. In the merit of the five things, our ancestors derived maximum benefit from the exile, by achieving its purpose of preventing assimilation with the gentiles, and thus they were fit to be redeemed.

The purpose of the bondage, was also for Israel's benefit. In Egypt, the Jews developed the trait of servitude. When they left Egypt and accepted the Torah, it was easy for them to fulfill the mitzvot. They simply directed the trait of servitude towards serving Hashem and obeying His commands.

Similarly, the Gemara[22] relates that a gentile said to Hillel, "Convert me on condition that you teach me the entire Torah on one foot." Hillel told him, "What is hateful to you, do not do to your friend. This is the entire Torah; the rest is commentary. Go learn." Rashi explains that the "friend" is Hashem, and Hillel was saying: You hate it when your friend transgresses your words, so don't you transgress Hashem's Word.

---

21. *Hagigah* 5b.
22. *Shabbat* 31a.

This well-known anecdote may be explained as follows. The gentile wished to develop one trait that would make it easier for him to fulfill all the mitzvot. Hillel told him to develop love for others. This trait can easily be directed toward loving Hashem, which in turn will make it easy to keep His mitzvot.

By acquiring the trait of servitude, and then directing it to serving Hashem by fulfilling His two mitzvot of Pesach and circumcision, our ancestors derived maximum benefit from the bondage, achieved its purpose, and could thus be redeemed.

But all this was only a preparation for the wonderful climax.

At the Burning Bush, Hashem told Moshe, "When you take the people out of Egypt, you will serve God on this mountain."[23] The redemption culminated at Mount Sinai, with the "marriage" of the Jewish people to Hashem, when we became His chosen people and received His Torah.

In the parable of the king and the poor woman, she needed to bring him a dowry to cement the bond between them, and the two earrings were enough. In the marriage between Hashem and Israel, the dowry that cements our connection is our *gedolim*. They are treasured, and through them, the Jewish nation becomes "My treasure out of all nations...."[24]

In summary, when Avraham asked in what merit his children would inherit the Land, Hashem unfolded a threefold process: Avraham's children would go into exile in order to become proud Jews. They would gain experience with servitude in order to become servants of Hashem. And He would give them leaders who would raise them to the level of Hashem's chosen people.

---

23. Shemot 3:12.
24. Shemot 19:5.

AHARON'S STAFF VERSUS EGYPT'S SORCERERS

Aaron cast down his staff before Pharaoh... and it became a serpent.
Pharaoh, too, summoned his wise men and his sorcerers.... Each one
cast down his staff and they became serpents. Then Aharon's staff swal-
lowed their staffs. (Shemot 7:10–12)

The Midrash[25] relates that Pharaoh made fun of Moshe and
Aharon. Cackling like a hen, he said to them, "These are the signs
of your God? Don't you know that all sorcery is in my domain?"
He sent for kindergarteners and they were able to do so, he then
summoned his wife, and she was also able to do so.

Why did Hashem introduce Himself to Pharaoh with a sign
that even Egyptian women and children could duplicate?

The answer can be found in the passage itself: "Then Aharon's
staff swallowed their staffs." Hashem's whole purpose was to hint
at the plagues, against which the Egyptians would not be able
to protect themselves, just as they could not protect their staffs
against Aharon's staff.

But Pharaoh missed the point. He thought it was a competition in magic, so he brought little children to produce magic.
Even after Aaron's staff swallowed theirs, he didn't understand
the message. Later, during the first two plagues, Pharaoh brought
sorcerers to turn water into blood and bring forth frogs, although
by doing so he hurt the Egyptians even more.

Imagine Reuven hits Shimon with a stick, and in response
Shimon brags, "I can do it, too," and hits himself with a stick.

This is how Pharaoh acted. In fact, his behavior was so absurd
that, "Hashem commanded them... concerning Pharaoh,"[26] which
Rashi explains that Hashem had to command Moshe and Aharon

---

25. *Shemot Rabbah* 9:6.
26. Shemot 6:13.

to treat Pharaoh with respect. Surely these tzaddikim spoke respectfully even to the simplest of men as required by *derech eretz*.[27] Yet they had to be warned to treat the king with respect because his reactions were so illogical and frustrating.

What prevented Pharaoh from catching on?

Gaavah — arrogance.

Much later, when the plagues were ravaging Egypt, even arrogant Pharaoh should have been smart enough to release the Jews and save his country. Why didn't he?

To answer, let's look at the Plague of Hail, when Moshe warned the Egyptians to take their servants and livestock inside or they would die. "Whoever of Pharaoh's servants feared Hashem's word chased his servants and his livestock to the houses. But whoever did not take God's word to heart left his servants and livestock in the field."[28] According to Targum Yonatan, it was Iyov who heeded the warning, while Bilaam and his disciples did not.

Why weren't they afraid of the financial loss? After all, in the six preceding plagues, all of Moshe's warnings came true!

A cosmic war was being waged between the Side of Good and Holiness, and the Side of Evil and Impurity. Heeding Moshe's warning would mean surrendering and losing the war. So Bilaam — impurity personified — urged the Egyptians not to heed despite the financial loss.

The Torah relates that together with the sorcerers, Pharaoh summoned "the wise men." The sorcerers made magic, while the wise men — Bilaam and his disciples — pushed for fighting the Side of Good at all costs. The *Zohar*[29] relates that Pharaoh listened to their advice because Hashem had hardened his heart; but

---

27. Refined behavior.
28. Shemot 9:20 –21.
29. Parashat Bo.

when his firstborn died, he took his sword and slew the wise men.

Amalek acted like the Egyptians. When the Jews left Egypt, "Nations heard and were agitated; terror gripped the dwellers of Philistia ...."[30] Yet one nation set out to weaken the impact the departure from Egypt had made on the world. Amalek came to fight Israel, although he knew he would be hurt in the battle.

And to this very day, the Side of Evil continues to wage a suicidal campaign against the Side of Good.

THE PLAGUE OF FROGS

"The Nile shall swarm with frogs, and they shall ascend and come into your palace... and into your ovens and your kneading bowls." (Shemot 7:19)

The Gemara[31] expounds: What did Hananiah, Mishael, and Azariah see to give up their lives in sanctification of the Name in the burning oven? They learned from the frogs. They said: If the frogs, who were not commanded to sanctify Hashem's Name, went into the oven, we, who are commanded to sanctify the Name, should certainly do so!

How could Hananiah, Mishael, and Azariah say that unintelligent frogs intended to sanctify the Name? The nature of the frog is to jump, and those near the oven automatically jumped in!

We can answer on the basis of the Midrash,[32] which says: The noise of the frogs was worse than the frogs themselves. They entered the Egyptians' bodies and shouted inside them, as it is written, "concerning the occurrence of the frogs" and the words the Torah

---

30. Shemot 15:14–15.
31. *Pesahim* 53b.
32. *Shemot Rabbah* 10:6.

uses are *al devar hatzfarde'im,*[33] which can also be translated "about the speech of the frogs." The frogs had to have intelligence in order to speak so we can conclude that miraculously, intelligence was bestowed on them.

Another Midrash[34] says that Hashem attacked the Egyptians with standard military strategy. First He cut off their water supply by turning the waters into blood. When they did not repent, He sent in soldiers — the frogs, who entered the city to execute justice.

Thus like soldiers entering a city, the frogs shouted and threatened with words.

These speaking, thinking frogs could have fled from the oven, but instead they chose to sanctify Hashem's Name by jumping in. Hananiah, Mishael, and Azariah, too, could have fled.[35] But they chose to stay and be thrown into the burning oven to sanctify His Name.

---

33. About the matter of the frogs (Shemot 8:8).
34. *Yalkut Shimoni* 182,
35. See Tosafot, *Pesahim* 53b.

PARASHAT

Bo

KORBAN PESACH

"Draw and take for yourselves a lamb for your families, and slaughter the Pesach offering." (Shemot 12:21)

Rather than carry the lamb for the Pesach offering over their shoulders, the Jews were to drag it through the streets, then barbecue it, filling the air with a strong, unmistakable aroma. To top it off, they were to keep its bones identifiably intact. The Egyptians would see their deity dragged ignominiously, smell it being barbecued, and then see its bones rolling around in the streets.

Why did the Jews have to provoke the Egyptians? What benefit for *avodat Hashem*[1] could possibly come of it?

We may answer in light of the Rambam's[2] statement that a person is naturally drawn after his friends and his countrymen. If his friends and countrymen are wicked, he should dwell alone. We can understand that a person is influenced by his friends, whom he consults or socializes with, since he hears their opinions. But how can he be influenced by countrymen outside his social circle?

Rabbi Yeruham explained[3] that a person naturally craves

---

1. Service of Hashem.
2. *Hilchot De'ot*, ch. 6.
3. Heard by the author.

recognition from society at large. In order to get it, he adheres to its norms and does what it deems important. If he lives in India, for instance, he is liable to start honoring cows, which is part of an idolatrous practice. To avoid such things, Rambam tells him to "dwell alone" — that is, stay home.

In order to leave Egypt, the Jews had to disconnect from its culture. The laws of the Pesach offering, from dragging the lamb through the street, to slaughtering, barbecuing, and eating it, were meant to break the connection. Thus, "and I said to you, 'In your bloods, live!'"[4] — refers to the blood of the Pesach offering and to the blood of circumcision;[5] both mitzvot were performed on that fateful night. And that night, they were to stay home, as commanded: "No man shall go out of the door of his house until morning."[6]

Only by disconnecting from the alien culture did we become redeemable then. And only by disconnecting from the alien culture will we become redeemable today.

THE FOUR SONS

It will be when you come into the land that Hashem will give you as he said He would, and you will perform this service [of the Korban Pesach.] And when your sons say to you, "What is this service that you are performing?"

You shall say, "It is a Pesach offering to Hashem, Who passed over the houses of Benei Yisrael when He smote the Egyptians, but He saved our households." (Shemot 12:25–27)

The Pesach Hagadah, which we recite at the Seder, tells us that the Torah speaks of four types of sons, the wise son, the wicked

---

4. Yehezkel 16:6.
5. Rashi on Shemot 12:6.
6. Shemot 12:22.

son, the simple son and the son who doesn't know to ask. It then presents the questions of the first three as recorded in the Torah. However the answers are not necessarily the answers recorded in the Torah. Why is this so?

Because a father is required to understand his children so well that he will know how to answer each one appropriately as we will explain.

Hacham — The Wise Son

The question asked in the Torah is, "What are the... laws... that Hashem, our God, commanded?"[7] To which the Torah answers, "We were slaves to Pharaoh in Egypt, and Hashem took us out with a strong hand."[8]

However, the Hagadah answers, "Instruct him in the laws of the Pesach offering...."

This question can be asked on two levels. He may want to know the laws so that he can fear Hashem and obey Him, as each Jew must. Or, he may want to know the *taamei hamitzvot*,[9] so that he can serve Hashem with love and a deep appreciation for the mitzvoth. A father must understand his son to discern his question. If he only wants to know the laws then answers him as the Hagadah says, telling him all the laws. However, if he wants to learn to that he can serve Hashem on the higher level of love he explains to him the, reasons for the mitzvah as the Torah says: "We were slaves to Pharaoh in Egypt, and Hashem took us out with a strong hand."

---

7. Devarim 6:20.
8. Devarim 6:1.
9. The "tastes" — an appreciation for the "reasons" behind the mitzvot. The real reason for any mitzvah, however, is that Hashem so commanded.

Rasha — The Wicked Son

The question asked in the Torah is, "What is this *avodah* to you?" To which the Torah answers, "It is a Pesach offering to Hashem...." However, the Hagadah answers, "Blunt his teeth and say to him, 'It is for the sake of this that Hashem did for me when I left Egypt'[10] — *for me*, not for him; had he been there, he would not have been redeemed."

The son who asks, "What is this *avodah* for you?", seems to consider mitzvah observance "work" (*avodah*) rather than a privilege[11] and says that mitzvoth are "for you" but not "for me." This seems to imply that he is wicked. However, he might just need gentle guidance to bring him back on the right course.

Therefore the Torah doesn't tell the father to condemn him, rather to treat him like the *hacham,* and speak to him about the Pesach offering.

But if after studying his nature carefully, his father realizes that he is truly wicked then he must be handled as the Hagadah says, "Blunt his teeth and say to him, 'It is for the sake of this that Hashem did *for me* when I left Egypt'[12] — for me, not for him."

She'eno Yodea Lishol — The Son Who Does Not Know How to Ask

The Torah records no question and no answer, however the Hagadah answers, "It is for the sake of this that Hashem did for me when I left Egypt."

If a son is silent, the father must understand why he isn't asking. Is it because he doesn't know how to ask a deep question,[13] or

---

10. Shemot 13:8.
11. *Yerushalmi.*
12. Shemot 13:8.
13. Rashi, Shemot 13:14.

is it because he doesn't care about the mitzvot? In other words, is he a *she'eno yodea lishol* or is he a *rasha*? The Hagadah tells us to quote him the verse where the Torah tells us about the Exodus from Mitzraim but at the same time hinting the answer to the wicked son — because he may be wicked.

Tam — The Simple Son

The question asked in the Torah is, "What is this?"[14] to which the Torah and the Hagadah both answer, "With a strong hand Hashem took us out of Egypt...."[15]

Only one son — the *tam* — is straightforward to deal with, however, the father must be sure that this son is a *tam* before treating him like one.

What is a *tam*? Yaakov Avinu is called an *ish tam yoshev ohalim,* a *tam* man abiding in tents [of Torah].[16] Rashi explains that a *tam* is one whose heart is like his mouth. He says what he means and he means what he says. Targum explains *tam* to mean, perfect. He does the right thing at the right time, living by the Torah and not deviating right or left.

All four sons are discussed on the Seder night, which is the night for passing our heritage down to the next generation. To succeed in *hinuch,* parents must know each child well and educate each one in the right way for him or her. Then, when they grow up, they won't say, "Dad and Mom never understood me."

Our children are also our disciples, and vice versa. It is told that a *rebbe* of young boys once asked Rabbi Ben-Tzion Abba Shaul to bless him with success in *hinuch.* The blessing he received

---

14. Shemot 13:14.
15. Ibid.
16. Bereshit 25:27.

was "May it be His will that you merit to truly understand the children."

Rabbi Natan Tzvi Finkel, the Elder of Slobodka, trained many great Torah scholars. His success is said to have come from understanding each disciple and knowing how to treat him — when to give compliments and when to give rebuke, when to show warmth and when to show coolness. Parents would do well to follow his lead.

THE *RASHA*'S QUESTION

"What is this *avodah* to you?"

Let's take another look at the *Rasha*'s question and the answers given. As mentioned above, the Torah treats him well, but the Hagadah treats him roughly. Here I would like to give a different explanation.

The question asked in the Torah is, "What is this *avodah* to you?" To which the Torah answers, "It is a Pesach offering to Hashem...." However, the Hagadah answers, "Blunt his teeth and say to him, 'It is for the sake of this that Hashem did for me when I left Egypt'[17] — *for me*, not for him; had he been there, he would not have been redeemed."

The Torah is speaking of a son who asked this question before the Torah was given. Then it was not so terrible to call the mitzvot *avodah*, "work." But afterwards, doing so makes the person a *rasha*. Why?

When the Torah was given, Hashem said to the Jewish people, "You shall be to Me a kingdom of priests and a holy nation."[18] From then on, every Jewish man is a king; every Jewish woman, a queen.

---

17. Shemot 13:8.
18. Shemot 19:6.

Royalty has protocols, and ours are the mitzvot. A monarch is strict about every detail of the royal protocols. To him, they are not a burden, but a privilege that comes with his elevated status.

BORROWING GOLD AND SILVER

Before Israel left Egypt, Hashem commanded Moshe to have the Jews borrow from the Egyptians gold and silver, telling him, *"Daber na, Speak, please, in the ears of the people: Let each man request of his fellow... silver vessels and gold vessels."* (Shemot 11:2)

The Midrash says:

Na means please. Hashem said to Moshe: Please, go and tell Israel: Please, let each man request of his fellow, silver vessels and gold vessels, so that the tzaddik [Avraham, to whom Hashem had promised that Israel will leave Egypt with great riches,] will not say, "He fulfilled 'they will serve them, and they will oppress them,' but He did not fulfill 'afterwards they will leave with great wealth.'"[19]

Israel said to Moshe, "If only we would be able go out ourselves [without silver and gold]!"

The matter may be likened to the prisoner sitting in jail. People told him, "Tomorrow you will be released, and you will be given great wealth."

He told them, "Please release me today, even with nothing."

Why didn't the Jews want to borrow silver and gold from the Egyptians? And how did Hashem allay their qualms by speaking about his promise to Avraham?

We may explain as follows.

The Jews wanted to disconnect totally from Egypt. They were afraid that borrowing from the Egyptians would keep them connected.

---

19. Bereshit 15:14.

Hashem explained that they were not borrowing, but asking for payment due for decades of slave labor. This He had promised Avraham: "They will serve them," and "afterwards they will leave with great wealth" in payment for their work.

If so, why did Hashem want them to approach the Egyptians by asking to borrow?

This, too, was part of the perfectly orchestrated Divine plan. After the Jews left, the Egyptians would pursue them in order to take back their silver and gold. Then Hashem would drown the Egyptians in the sea for throwing Jewish babies into the Nile — exquisite measure-for-measure retribution,

*　　　*　　　*

There is yet another reason that the Jews did not want the wealth.

Hashem's request to borrow silver and gold came after the Plague of Darkness. The Midrash[20] says that some of the Jews, who had Egyptian patrons, were wealthy and honored and did not want to leave Egypt. Hashem brought darkness upon Egypt in order to kill these sinners without their enemies seeing.

But the other Jews saw that money, expensive furniture, and the latest-model horse-driven carriages made it hard for a person to leave Egypt. They were afraid to take wealth from the Egyptians lest it bring them to ruin as it had ruined those sinners.

Hashem said to them: From silver and gold you can build a Mishkan.[21] Take it now with the intention of fulfilling My statement, "Afterwards they will leave with great wealth." Even Avraham agreed to it, for if you use wealth for mitzvot, you will not stumble.

*　　　*　　　*

---

20. *Bereshit Rabbah* 14:3.
21. Sanctuary.

When the Jews left Egypt, the Torah says, *Vayenatzlu et Mitz-rayim,* "They emptied Egypt"[22] — the Gemara explains this to mean that they made it like a trap (*metzudah*) without grain and like the depths of the sea (*metzulah*) without fish.[23] What is the significance of these metaphors?

Before this, Egypt had resembled a fisherman who uses grain to bait fish. This land of prosperity and opportunity attracted people from all over — and then trapped them and didn't let them leave. After the Jews emptied Egypt of its wealth, there was nothing left there to attract people; there was no bait, and so there were no fish.

Hashem did this for the benefit of the Jewish people — to reduce their temptation to return to Egypt. And for extra measure, He impoverished the land even more after they left, when Pharaoh emptied his treasuries to persuade his soldiers to pursue the Jews.

22. Shemot 12:36.
23. *Berachot* 9b.

PARASHAT

Beshalah

PROVIDING AN ESCORT

When the Jews left Egypt it says, Vayehi beshalah, *When Pharaoh sent out the people...* (Shemot 13:17)

This is the usual translation, but Midrash Rabbah objects: Did Pharaoh send them out? Didn't God take them out as Bilaam said, "God took them out of Egypt"[1]?

Midrash Rabbah solves the problem by translating: *Vayehi beshalah,* to mean, When Pharaoh escorted the people, as we find the word *beshalah* meaning "escorted" in reference to Avraham escorting the angels, where it says, And Avraham went with them *lishalchom*.[2] Nevertheless, the usual word for "escort" is *livui,* why did the Torah use the word *beshalah*? The Tanhuma answers that Pharaoh used the word *shalach* when he said, "I will *not* send them out" so now he retracted and said, "I *will* send them out."

The Tanhuma continues that for this he was rewarded that the Torah tells us, "You shall not abominate an Egyptian."[3]

But why was Pharaoh rewarded for escorting them? After all

---

1. Bamidbar 24:8.
2. *VeAvraham holech imam leshalham* (Bereshit 18:16).
3. Devarim 23:8.

Pharaoh only wanted to hurry the Jews out, as the Torah says: "Egypt strongly hurried the people to send them out of the land, for they said, 'We are all dying!'"[4] ,

We may find the answer in the laws of charity. Suppose Reuven gives charity with the intention that his sick son be healed in its merit, or even with no intention at all — a coin fell from his pocket and was found by a pauper. In both cases, Reuven is accredited with the mitzvah of charity. Regardless of Reuven's intentions, bottom line a Jew benefited from his money.

Although Pharaoh's intention was to hurry the Jews, bottom line he escorted them. The sight of the mighty king escorting them gave the Jews a good feeling — and giving them a good feeling brought Pharaoh great reward.

The mitzvah of escorting a guest four cubits — just a few steps — when he leaves your home is very powerful![5] In fact, our Sages said that failing to escort is akin to bloodshed. The Rambam[6] writes that the reward for escorting is greater than for all acts of kindness. It's a law that Avraham Avinu enacted in the world. He himself served passers-by food and then escorted them, and the escorting meant more than the serving.

When I was a yeshiva student, alone in the United States, Rabbi Naftali Friedler regularly invited me to his home for Shabbat. On Motzaei Shabbat, he would escort me to the elevator, and I'll never forget the good feeling it gave me.

If a guest leaves your home and you accompany him a few steps, you will reap huge benefits.

---

4. Shemot 12:33.
5. See *Sotah* 46b.
6. *Hilchot Avelut* 14:2–3.

EMUNAH

After the Red Sea split, Yisrael saw the great hand that Hashem inflicted on Egypt, and the people feared Hashem, and they believed in Hashem and in Moshe, His servant.(Shemot 13:31)

Did the Jews only believe in Hashem now after the sea split? Hadn't they had already believed when Moshe first brought them Hashem's word, and surely even more so after witnessing the Ten Plagues? What additional *emunah* did they acquire at the sea?

I would answer as follows.

Although the Jews already believed in Hashem, some things He did puzzled them. Why did He have Moshe ask Pharaoh to let the Jews leave Egypt for only three days? Why did He instruct them to "borrow" gold and silver from the Egyptians as if they were going to return it? Finally, why did He make the Jews journey backward returning towards Egypt after they had travelled into the desert?

At the sea, suddenly everything became clear, for they realized that all the puzzling things were a Divine plan to bring the Egyptians to the sea and drown them. They saw that with precise measure-for-measure retribution, Hashem drowned the Egyptians in the sea for having thrown the Jewish babies into the Nile.

They saw that Hashem deliberately misled the Egyptians into thinking that the Jews were only going out for a short holiday — so that when they failed to return, the Egyptians would get angry and pursue them. Then, to allay the Egyptians' fears, He had instructed the Jews to journey backward and encamp near the idol Baal Tzefon — so that Pharaoh would say, "They are lost in the desert and can't find their way out."[7] Trusting in Baal Tzefon

---

7. Shemot 14:3.

to protect the Egyptians and bring them victory, Pharaoh would bring his army to the sea.

It would have made more sense for Pharaoh to stay home and rebuild his land from the ravages of the Ten Plagues. Instead, he took the bait and made a laughingstock of himself.

Midrash Rabbah compares him to the servant who was sent by his master to buy a fish. The servant returned with one that was spoiled. Said the master, "Choose your punishment. Either eat the fish, receive a hundred lashes, or pay me a hundred dollar fine."

The servant chose to eat the fish. Halfway through, he could no longer bear it, and asked for the lashes; halfway through the lashes, he could no longer bear them and he ended up paying the money. Thus he wound up with all three punishments.

Ramban[8] writes: The Egyptians saw the sea split for the Jews and saw them walk through it on dry land. It is incomprehensible that after seeing this, the Egyptians would recklessly pursue them into the sea! This was the greatest of all wonders — that Hashem numbed their minds and strengthened their desire to enter the sea.

Seeing this great wonder, the Jews acquired a greater belief in Hashem and in Moshe, His servant.

Herein lies a powerful lesson for us in *emunah*. Even when everything seems to be going wrong; everything is going exactly according to Hashem's plan, and for our ultimate good.

BUILDING A TEMPLE

After the splitting of the Red Sea the Jews sang a song to Hashem. In this song they proclaimed, *This is my God,* ve'anvehu. (Shemot 15:2)

---

8. Shemot 14:4.

What is meant by *ve'anvehu*?

Rashi gives two explanations. The first is, "I will make myself beautiful before Him with mitzvot", teaching us the concept of *hidur mitzvah*.[9] With this proclamation the Jews undertook willingly, of their own volition, to beautify the mitzvot they perform — to make beautiful Torah Scrolls, beautiful tefillin, and so on.

The second interpretation follows Onkelos' translation, "I will build Him a Temple." Meaning the Jews accepted on themselves to build a Temple for Hashem. But this raises a question. Since building the Temple is a mitzvah, why did the Jews need to promise to do it? After all, when we are commanded to fulfill any mitzvah, be it building a Temple or anything else, we simply do it.

We can answer this question in light of the well-known story about two brothers who jointly owned a field. One had a large family; the other was still a bachelor. When they harvested the wheat, each took half. Afterwards the married brother said to himself, "How can I take half for myself? My brother will need a lot of money to get married!" So late that night, he took part of his own wheat and headed stealthily toward the bachelor's domain.

Meanwhile the bachelor said to himself, "How can I take half for myself? My brother has a family to feed!" So late that night, he, too, took part of his own wheat and headed stealthily toward his brother's domain.

In the middle of the way, the brothers met each other. Each was touched by the other's concern, and they embraced. At that moment, Hashem said, "Here is where the Temple will be built." For the Shechinah rests only where there is unity, where each one thinks how to help the other.

---

9. Beautifying a mitzvah.

Thus the mitzvah to build the Temple is not enough. The essence of the Temple is for the Shechinah to rest on it, and that depends on the unity of the Jewish people. At the sea, when they sang *Shirah,* the time was right for saying, "I will build Him a Temple" — I will think of others, so that the Shechinah can have a dwelling place. For at a time of joy, the heart is open to making such a promise.

Midrash Rabbah[10] says:

> Moshe Rabbenu asked, "Is it possible to build a house for the Shechinah?"
>
> Hashem replied, "Even one person can build it," thus it is written, "From every man whose heart motivates him you shall take My portion."[11]

How does this verse prove that one person can build a Temple? One person didn't build it alone; he joined with others!

That is precisely the point. When people join together harmoniously, they can build a Temple, and it is considered as if each one built it.

And what is the purpose of the Temple?

We might think it is to atone for the Jewish people through sacrifices. But on the verse "They shall make for me a Temple, and I will dwell inside them,"[12] our Sages note: It does not say "inside it" but "inside them" — inside every single one. Accordingly, the main purpose of the Temple is to serve as a model for every Jewish home. Thus at the sea, each Jew said, "This is my God, and I will build Him a Temple" — in my own home.

---

10. *Ot* 8.
11. Shemot 25:2.
12. Shemot 25:8.

Midrash Rabbah[13] explains the purpose of the Temple with a parable about a king who had an only daughter. A prince from another land came and wed her. When the prince wanted to return to his land, the king told him, "I have given you my only daughter, but I cannot part with her. Do me a favor. Wherever you go, make me a small room so that I can live with you." Similarly, Hashem said to the Jewish people, "I have given you the Torah, but I cannot part with it. Please make Me a house so that I can live with you." Thus it is written, "They shall make Me a Temple."

The parable teaches us that the Temple's main purpose is to model the building of a Jewish home, and that in a Jewish home, the Torah should guide every step.

In the Temple there were common items found in every home, such as meat, bread, wine, salt, and water. But the Tablets of the Covenant and the Torah were in in the Inner Sanctum, which transformed, uplifted, and sanctified everything in the Temple. In our homes, too, the inner core must be Torah, which transforms, uplifts, and sanctifies everything in the home.

In the Temple, atonement came through sacrifices. At home, it comes through our table, as our Sages teach. We may explain this based on the Gemara[14] that says, "He who allows himself to be persuaded through wine has within him some of his Creator's wisdom." This may be understood as follows: Suppose Reuven offended Shimon and after regretting it, offers Shimon some wine. If Shimon accepts the wine and forgives, he displays that he has some wisdom of his Creator. For Hashem, too, forgives us when we bring him a sacrifice along with wine for *nesachim*.

Thus the Temple teaches us what to do even if the unity has

---

13. *Shemot Rabbah* 33:1.
14. *Eruvin* 65a.

been disrupted. Don't bear a grudge. Forgive and forget, and restore the harmony.

THE MANNA

While the Jews travelled in the desert, Hashem fed them with heavenly bread. *Benei Yisrael saw and they said to one another, Man hu, "What is this?"*[15] *for they did not know what it was. Moshe said to them, "This is the bread that Hashem has given you to eat."* (Shemot 16:15)

Moshe said, "This is the thing that Hashem has commanded: A full measure of it shall be a safekeeping for your generations, so that they will see the bread I fed you in the desert when I took you out of the land of Egypt." ...Aaron placed it before the Ark of Testimony for a safekeeping. (Shemot 16:32–34)

In the first passage, why does the holy Torah record their seemingly insignificant talk? And what was the point of keeping the *man* for safekeeping mentioned in the second passage?

Rashi comments that the purpose of keeping the *man*[16] as a safekeeping was to encourage Yirmiyahu's generation which was several centuries later. When the prophet would rebuke the people for not studying Torah, they would counter, "If we stop working and study Torah, what will we eat?" Yirmiyahu would then take out the jar of *man* and say, "See, this is what your forefathers ate. Hashem has many means of preparing food for those who fear Him."

How is this an answer? Had Hashem given *man* to Yirmiyahu's generation, they surely would have studied Torah full time, but since He didn't, how could they be expected to eat if they didn't work?

---

15. Translation follows *Ohr HaHayyim.*
16. Manna.

With one idea we can answer all these questions.

Says the *Ohr HaHayyim*: The usual way of asking "What is this?" is *Mah hu*. But when the Jews first saw the bread from heaven, Hashem inspired them to express themselves by saying, *Man hu,* which can also be interpreted as "it is *man*" because *man* is its true name. Similarly, we know that parents are Divinely inspired to name their newborn the name G-d gave to the newborn's soul.[17]

We can figure out why Hashem called it *man*, by studying the *man*.

The Torah relates that regardless of how much a person gathered, when he opened his basket at home he found the same measure. Thus whoever gathered more, toiled in vain.

The Gemara[18] adds that the righteous had their *man* delivered to their doorstep, the middle-of-the-road people found it in the camp, while the wicked found it outside the camp. Additionally, the righteous found ready-to-eat bread; the middle-of-the-road people found dough, which required baking; and the wicked had to grind their *man* into flour and continue from there.

How can the Gemara talk about wicked people in the desert, who was wicked Jews in the desert? No one desecrated Shabbat except for Datan and Aviram, who once went out to gather *man*, and the wood gatherer, who sinned once for the sake of heaven.

I would suggest that here the terms "righteous" and "wicked" used here don't refer to righteous and wicked people rather it refers to the different levels of *bitahon,* trust in Hashem, that they had. *Bitahon* also means confidence and security. The righteous of the desert trusted fully in Hashem and relied on Him to provide

---

17. See *Berachot* 7b, which expounds: *Asher sam shamot baaretz* (Tehilim 46:9) — "Who places names (*shemot*) in the land."
18. *Yoma* 72a.

all their needs. The peace of mind that characterizes *bitahon*[19] made them calm and confident, as in "The righteous are confident as a young lion."[20] The wicked of the desert, who lacked *bitahon*, were agitated. Rearranging the letters of רשע (*rasha*), "wicked," yields רעש (*raash*), "tumult." The wicked were tumultuous and agitated, as in "The wicked are like the driven sea that cannot rest."[21]

Often, when people woke up, they were surprised to see someone, who appeared to be distinguished, having to trudge far from his tent to gather his *man*, while the *man* of a simple person was waiting on his doorstep. Everything depended on *bitahon*, the less one had, the harder he needed to work, the more he had, the less effort he required — merely stepping out of his tent to take the *man* sufficed.[22]

The same principle applies today.

Bitahon does not come automatically; it requires preparation. As *Hovot HaLevavot* says, we must train our thoughts to know that we will have exactly what Hashem has designated for us, regardless of how much we work.

The white color of the *man*[23] taught *bitahon*, for our Sages explain that it whitened the sins of Yisrael.[24] Rashi explains that they worried that *man* might not fall the next day, so they subjugated their hearts to Hashem.

But if the *man* made them worry that Hashem might not provide for them, it should have blackened their sins! How can we understand Rashi?

I would venture to answer that because they worried that the

---

19. See *Hovot HaLevavot, Shaar HaBitahon*, ch. 1.
20. *Mishlei* 28:1.
21. Yeshayahu 57:20.
22. See *Bet HaLevi*, Parashat Miketz.
23. Shemot 16:31.
24. *Yoma* 75a.

next day their *man* might fall further away, they were compelled to continually work on their *bitahon*.

This can be illustrated by the following scenario: Hayyim visited Shalom and grumbled, "What will be? When will we finally enter the Promised Land?" Shalom afraid that these words might weaken his own *bitahon* immediately begins working on preparing *bitahon*, strengthening his own belief that Hashem always does what is best for us.

Since what kind of *man* fell and where it fell depended on a person's *bitahon* preparations, Hashem named it "preparation." For *man* means preparation, as in *vayeman Hashem dag*, "Hashem prepared a large fish to swallow Yonah."[25] Rashi,[26] too, explains *man* as preparation, albeit of food. The Torah right after detailing the laws of Shabbat, relates that "the house of Yisrael called it *man*"[27] because both *man* and Shabbat depend on preparation. What a person will get out of Shabbat depends on how he prepares for it.

Now we can explain how displaying the *man* encouraged the people of Yirmiyahu's generation to study Torah. The prophet was telling them — and us: Look at the *man*, which fell for each person according to his level of trust in Hashem. The *man* teaches that the more *bitahon* you prepare and develop, the less time you will need for work, and the more time you will have for Torah study.

---

25. Yonah 2:1.
26. Shemot 16:15.
27. Shemot 16:31.

Yitro

YITRO PRAISES HASHEM

Yitro, the priest of Midian, the father-in-law of Moshe, heard every-thing that God did to Moshe and to Yisrael, His people — that Hashem had taken them out of Egypt. (Shemot 18:1)

Rashi, citing the *Mechilta,* says:

And Yitro heard — What did Yitro hear that prompted him to come? The splitting of the Sea of Reeds and the war of Amalek.

Why does Rashi say that Yitro heard only two things? After all, the verse itself says that Yitro heard, *everything that God did,* which Rashi himself explains to mean, the manna, the well, and [the victory over] Amalek!

To answer the question, let's examine Yitro's coming.

Yitro did not enter Moshe's tent, or even the camp of Yisrael. He stayed out of the camp and sent a messenger to inform Moshe that he had arrived. Thereupon "Moshe went out to meet his father-in-law."[1] The Midrash says that Yitro was accorded great honor at that time, because after seeing Moshe go out, Aharon went out with Nadav and Avihu; and seeing their leaders going out, everyone followed suit.

---

1. Shemot 18:7.

Why did Yitro behave in this way? He could easily have found Moshe's tent. Why did he trouble everyone to come and greet him?

And that's not all. After Moshe greeted him, Yitro asked Moshe to relate all the miracles. "Yitro rejoiced over all the good..., and said, *'Baruch Hashem,* Blessed is Hashem, Who rescued you....'"[2] Then Yitro made a great banquet to which he invited everyone. Why?

Yitro's actions were the product of deep thought and careful planning. Yitro knew that when Hashem split the sea, "peoples heard — they were agitated; terror gripped the inhabitants of Philistia."[3] The whole world was afraid of the Jews. Then Amalek came, jumped into the proverbial boiling pot, and cooled it off for the nations — and to some extent, for the Jews themselves.

What do you do in such a situation? You gather together for *hizuk*.[4] And that was precisely Yitro's plan. "Yitro, the father-in-law of Moshe, heard." Rashi notes that Yitro gloried in being Moshe's father-in-law. Why did Yitro need this glory when he came? So that everyone would come to greet him. Thus Yitro gathered the people together and gave a fiery *derashah*,[5] saying, "Now I know that Hashem is greater than all the gods, for in the very matter in which [the Egyptians] had conspired against them...!"[6]

These words had a powerful impact, coming as they did from a former advisor to Pharaoh, who knew exactly what the Egyptians were scheming and how Hashem had paid them back measure for measure. And Yitro surely continued: Just as Hashem punished Egypt, so will He punish Amalek!

---

2. Shemot 18:9–10.
3. Shemot 15:14.
4. Encouragement and spiritual strengthening.
5. Sermon.
6. Shemot 18:11.

It is told that when the Rosh Yeshiva of Hevron was a child, he saw a well-known tzaddik of Jerusalem standing in front of a notice that had been posted about folk dancing. The tzaddik read the notice and even copied down the date and time of the event. Noticing the child's astonishment, the tzaddik explained, "Whenever *hillul Hashem*[7] takes place in Jerusalem, we gather and learn Torah *lishmah* throughout that time in order to offset it."

Similarly, Yitro gave the Jews *hizuk* in order to offset the war of Amalek which cooled off the impact made by the splitting of the sea.

In addition, "Yitro rejoiced over all the good... and... said, '*Baruch Hashem.*" He also enthused over Hashem's kindness, and made a banquet to celebrate it.

Our Sages say it was a discredit to Moshe and the Jewish people that they hadn't said *Baruch Hashem*. But the Jews sang praise at the sea shouldn't that count more than two words of thanks? And if saying *Baruch Hashem* is so important, why didn't Moshe Rabbenu and the Jewish people say it?

The difference is that Yitro now heard a running account of all the miracles, and he was ecstatically excited. Yitro's *Baruch Hashem* was like David HaMelech's *Kosi revayah*[8] — Hashem gives me more and more until my cup overflows. The Jews, too, should have felt ecstatically excited and grateful as if all the miracles were happening together just then. Human nature is such that our excitement over miracles wanes with time, and we must fight to keep it fresh.

When we are asked, "How are you?" and we answer, "*Baruch Hashem,*" we must think, "Today things are going well, and that is

7. Desecration of Hashem's Name.
8. Tehilim 23:5.

besides all that Hashem did for me yesterday, and the day before, and the day before that... since I was born." That is why we say *Baruch Hashem* — to feel the great blessing, to thank Him for all the good.

To concretize this concept even further, Yitro invited everyone to a banquet. Thus he taught us to make a *se'udat hodayah*.[9]

If we must be enthusiastically grateful for Hashem's miracles and kindness, how much more must we be grateful for His Torah, which is the greatest good! A certain rabbi recalled that his father once came home and made a little party for the family, at which he gave out peanuts and almonds, because he had said a good *peshat*[10] in the Rashba that day. Love of Torah can only be given over with joy, and this father's love of Torah had a tremendous impact on his children.

A wealthy businessman who supported many yeshivot once asked Rav Shach, "Who has more in the world to come: you or me?"

Rav Shach replied, "In the world to come, your reward is very great. But in this world, I definitely have more. Nothing can compare to the pleasure I get from understanding a difficult Rambam!"

HASHEM'S TREASURED NATION

Ko tomar levet Yaakov vetaged livnei Yisrael, *Thus shall you say to the House of Yaakov and tell to Benei Yisrael...* (Shemos 19:3)

Rashi explains: The House of Yaakov are the women, to whom Moshe was to speak gently (*tomar*). Benei Yisrael are the men, to whom Moshe was to speak toughly (*taged*), telling them the punishments and *dikdukim*.

---

9. Festive meal to express gratitude to Hashem.
10. Explanation.

How could Moshe tell the men something different than the women, after all, the Torah spells out clearly the message Moshe was to convey: "You have seen what I did to Egypt.... And now, if you obey Me and keep My covenant, you shall be to Me the most beloved, precious treasure....[11] You shall be to Me a kingdom of priests and a holy nation."[12] And Hashem concludes: "These are the words that you shall speak to Benei Yisrael"[13] — no more and no less.[14]

Clearly, Hashem's message was pleasant and gentle. How could Moshe add "punishments and *dikdukim*" when speaking to the men?

We may answer, that there is a rule in the Torah, that the negative can be inferred from the positive (*miklal hen atah shome'a lav*). Thus the statement, *if you obey Me and keep My covenant, you shall be to Me the most beloved, precious treasure...*, also conveys that if we don't fulfill His Will, the opposite will happen and we will be handed over to a lowly nation — or, even worse, to its animals, as our Sages said. Moshe was to tell the men the punishments learned from *dikdukim* — careful analysis of the verses. But to the women, Moshe was to emphasize only the beauty of being a treasured nation, with all Jews being kings and queens.

Since men are tough, they are to be reminded of the severity of Divine punishment. Because of this, Rabbenu Tam would read the harsh punishments predicted in Parashat Ki Tavo every week. Similarly, in the yeshivot of pre-War Europe, if a student slacked off from his learning, they would say, "Hearty appetite" — hinting to the burning coals fed to a person after death for the sin of *bitul Torah*,[15] as our Sages teach.

---

11. Translation follows Rashi.
12. Shemot 19:4–6.
13. Shemot 19:6.
14. Rashi.
15. Neglect of Torah study.

Women, however, are to be treated gently. In Shir HaShirim, a metaphorical description of the love between Hashem and the Jewish people, the husband extols his wife. Even the metaphor is meaningful, and it teaches Jewish men to extol their wives. Praising, appreciating, and honoring one's wife are part of speaking gently to the House of Yaakov.

At his wife's funeral, Rav Shelomo Zalman Auerbach said, "Generally at a funeral one asks forgiveness. But I feel no need to do so here. Throughout our long marriage, neither of us ever hurt the other."

People wondered how that was possible, until a young man said, "I once accompanied the Rav home. Before we entered the house, the Rav stopped to adjust his hat and coat. Figuring that the Rav had guests, I wanted to leave so as not to disturb. But the Rav said, 'Don't go; I have no guests. But I do have a queen at home, and I must prepare myself to meet the queen.'"

"You shall be to Me a kingdom of priests" is more than the bestowal of a title. It is a command to treat our fellow Jew like royalty. When we arrive at the heavenly court, say our Sages, we will be asked, "Did you make your friend king over you pleasantly?" Thus the Vilna Gaon wrote to his wife, "Honor your mother-in-law"! In truth, if not for the fact that it isn't customary to do so, we should salute every Jew we meet as one salutes a king.

We should also treat ourselves as royalty and rejoice in our own kingship.

A yeshiva student woke up one morning singing and dancing. When asked what happened, he explained that he had heard that one morning Napoleon woke up and danced for joy saying, "The king of France got up and will keep the country running! Is that not cause for joy?" So too, when a yeshiva student gets up in the morning to pray and learn Torah he should think, "I am keeping the whole universe running! Is that not cause for joy?

THE TEN COMMANDMENTS

God spoke all these statements, saying....[16]

With the exception of Shabbat, the Ten Commandments apply to all of mankind. The commentators ask: Why don't they include laws given exclusively to the Jewish people, such as kashrut and *shatnez*?[17]

Furthermore, our Sages teach that Hashem offered the Torah to other nations but they declined it when they heard that the Torah forbids killing and stealing. How could Hashem have offered the Torah to other nations? After all, many of its laws commemorate the Jewish people's departure from Egypt! Similarly, the Torah forbids eating *gid hanasheh* because the angel touched the hip socket of Yaakov. Why should this apply to the descendants of Esav or Ishmael?

Perhaps Hashem's offer was only that they accept the Seven Noahide Laws by the command of Hashem and the Torah, and thereby merit the life of the world to come. But if so, why did they refuse because of the laws of killing and stealing, they also legislate laws against killing and stealing!

A different answer may be derived from the verse in Parashat Mishpatim: "Hashem said to Moshe, 'Ascend to Me to the mountain and remain there, and I shall give you the stone Tablets and the Torah and the mitzvah that I have written, to teach them.'"[18] Rashi comments: All 613 mitzvot are included in the Ten Commandments as worked out by Rabbenu Saadyah.

For instance, "You shall not kill" includes the prohibitions against handing a person over to the authorities for unjustified

---

16. Shemot 20:1.
17. Forbidden mixture of wool and linen.
18. Shemot 24:12.

execution, failing to save a person who is drowning if one is able to, and even speaking ill of another or embarrassing him in public. "You shall not commit adultery" includes the prohibitions against touching a woman who is forbidden to him, gazing at her, or being light-headed with her. "You shall not steal" includes the prohibition against *genevat daat*,[19] such as flattering a person by urging him be your guest when you know he will not accept.

When explaining the ten commandments, Targum Yonatan adds: "My people..., do not kill and do not be friends or partners of those who commit these sins, so that your children will not learn to do those deeds." Accordingly, a person who belongs to a group of sinners is considered a sinner himself.[20]

The gentiles did not want to accept the additional explanations of the Ten Commandments provided by Rabbenu Saadyah and Targum Yonatan. But we Jews declared, *Naaseh venishma*,[21] and willingly accepted the complete package.

---

19. Literally: Stealing of knowledge.
20. Similarly, regarding blessings the Gemara (*Pesahim* 102a) teaches that if a group eats a meal together, and a few leave with the intention of coming back, they are still considered part of the group.
21. We will do and we will hear.

PARASHAT
Mishpatim

EVED IVRI

And these are the laws that you shall place before them: If you buy an eved ivri,[1] he shall work for six years, and in the seventh he shall go free, for no charge. (Shemos 21:1-2)

Rashi explains that this passage is referring to a convicted thief whom the court sells as an *eved ivri*[2] to pay his debt. But this is hard to understand, who will buy him if the court tells the truth that he is a thief? People install locks to keep thieves out of their homes, why would they take in a thief?

Besides, why does the Torah begin the monetary laws with this topic? It should have begun with laws of *hesed*,[3] such as lending money[4] or returning lost things to their owners?[5]

The answer to these questions are that *eved ivri* is also about *hesed* on an exalted level. For, only a tsaddik, willing to dedicate himself selflessly to rehabilitate a person who has slipped up would take a convicted thief into his house. And not only that, the law is

---

1. Literally, Hebrew slave.
2. The following questions are asked by the commentators.
3. Loving-kindness.
4. Shemot 22:24.
5. Shemot 23:4.

that the Hebrew slave must be treated equal to the master, and if the master owns only one pillow or one portion of fresh bread and the like, he must give it to the *eved*. In other situations the laws of charity and *hesed* don't require such self-sacrifice.

The Torah instead of putting the thief in jail where he will learn from the other inmates and become a hardened criminal, is entrusted to a saintly master who will care for him gently, with sublime kindness, until he turns into a tzaddik.

Thus Parashat Mishpatim begins by teaching us to treat those who are not standard members of society with tremendous compassion. Our Torah leaders have always done just that.

For instance, the Gemara[6] relates that two men once made a wager over whether Hillel could be provoked to anger. One of them came to the Sage on Erev Shabbat and started asking him silly questions. Hillel, not only answered his questions, but even complimented him and encouraged him to ask more.

Finally, the fellow told Hillel that he had lost 400 *zuz* on his account. Hillel told him that it would have been worthwhile even to lose 800 *zuz* so that Hillel should not become angry. In other words, Hillel comforted him by explaining that his loss was actually a good investment: He had become part of a significant episode of human forbearance that would invoke Divine forbearance, measure for measure, upon the whole generation. In addition, the story would be recorded for posterity and inspire people to improve their *midot*.

Elsewhere the Gemara[7] relates that a man from the Land of Israel married a woman from Babylon, and their language differences caused misunderstandings. Once he asked her to bring two

---

6. Shabbat 31a.
7. *Nedarim* 66b.

butzina, which in his language meant watermelons, but in her language meant oil lamps. She brought oil lamps and he became angry. He told her to break the lamps on the *bava,* which in his language, meant the door, but she understood that he was telling her to break them on the head of the sage, Bava ben Buta. She went to the *bet midrash* and threw them on the Sage's head. Assumedly he thought she was unbalanced. Instead of becoming angry, he asked, "Why did you do that?" She replied, "I was following my husband's command." He said, "Since you did your husband's will, may Hashem give you two sons like Bava ben Buta."

In modern times, a tzaddik who treated unbalanced people with compassion was Rabbi Herman of New York's Lower East Side. His hospitality was legendary; he opened his house to everyone and anyone. One Shabbat, a guest threw his plate of *cholent* at the host. The other guests scolded him and he ran out of the house. His host ran after him, calling, "Come back, I'll give you another plate of *cholent!*" To people who praised this forbearance, Rabbi Herman said, "When you have compassion, you don't need forbearance."

People think that you lose when you are too giving, but the opposite is true. The proof is from Rahel Imenu. When her wily father substituted her sister, Leah, as Yaakov Avinu's bride, Rahel gave Leah the identifying signs to spare her embarrassment. It seemed that Rahel was forfeiting the privilege of becoming Yaakov's wife and the mother of the Shevatim. But our Sages say that Rahel was incapable of bearing children. Had she married Yaakov as planned, eventually he would have divorced her in order to produce the Shevatim. But she married Yaakov a week later, and because of her sublime *hesed,* say our Sages, Hashem granted her two sons. Rahel lost nothing and gained everything.

The more you give, the more you gain.

THE EAR THAT HEARD

If the eved *says, "I love my master...; I shall not go free," then his master shall bring him to the court... and bore through his ear with the awl, and he shall serve him forever.* (Shemot 21:5–6)

Rashi explains that if the *eved ivri* sold himself for money, his ear is bored because he heard with his own ear what was said at Sinai, "For unto Me are Benei Yisrael servants" — they are My servants, not servants of servants, and non-the-less he went and acquired a master for himself.

A few questions arise here. Why is the ear bored only in connection with the *eved* who didn't fulfill what he heard at Sinai, and not when one doesn't fulfill any other mitzvah given at Sinai?[8] In what way did the *eved* stop being a servant of Hashem? Even while he is an *eved* he is still obligated in all the mitzvot! If being an *eved* is wrong, why is he allowed to continue being an *eved*? If the ear is bored as a punishment it should be done by the court, which normally executes punishments, not by the master?

I heard Rabbi Naftali Friedler *zt"l* explain the psychology of this *eved*. The reason he wants to remain an *eved* is because he would rather rely on his master to feed him than have to rely on Hashem and look for a job, which he is afraid he may not find. But the Torah says that we are Hashem's servants, meaning that we must have *bitahon* in Him.

I would like add another reason. In order to please his master who feeds him, the *eved* will serve Hashem in his master's style, rather than in his own style. But the *Ohr HaHayyim* says that Hashem made people different, with everyone serving Hashem in his own style, in order to bring to fruition all seventy facets of the Torah.

---

8. Maharsha.

Thus the master is taking the *eved* to court to tell him not to place his trust in him, for he is only like the waiter who serves the food. People thank the waiter, but the food belongs to the master of the house. So too, we both are servants of Hashem, and He feeds all His servants. The master is boring his ear not as a punishment, but to be a constant reminder that "unto Me are Benei Yisrael servants."

When people came to the Hafetz Hayyim for a blessing, he would say, "Why turn to Me? Ask Hashem directly! The blessings don't come from me, but from Him." In the end, though, he would bless them.

Even when we ask a tzaddik for a blessing or we visit the graves of tzaddikim, we are turning only to Hashem, and merely asking the tzaddik to put in a good word for us.

PARASHAT

Terumah

THE POWER OF TORAH

The Torah begins the details of building the *Mishkan* saying, Veyikhu li terumah *And they shall take for Me a donation.* (Shemot 25:2) The literal translation of Veyikhu li terumah is "They shall take Me as a portion...."

The Gemara[1] relates that when Moshe went up to heaven to receive the Torah, the angels protested. "Master of the Universe," they said, "what is one born of woman doing among us?'

"He has come to receive the Torah," replied Hashem.

"Will You give this precious treasure, which You kept for 974 generations before the world was created, to flesh and blood? 'What is a human that You should remember him? Place Your glory above the heavens!'"[2]

Hashem told Moshe, "Answer them!"

"I fear they will burn me with the breath of their mouths," said Moshe.

Hashem told him, "Grasp the heavenly throne and answer them."

Said Moshe, "Look what is written in the Torah, 'I am Hashem... Who took you out of the land of Egypt.' Did you go down to Egypt?

1. *Shabbat* 89a.
2. Tehilim 8:2.

'Remember the Shabbat day to sanctify it.' Do you do work? 'Honor your father and your mother.' Do you have a father or mother?"

They immediately acknowledged that Moshe was right....

This Gemara is puzzling. Why did the angels want the Torah? Didn't they knew they couldn't keep it?

To answer the question, let's study a Midrash on our verse. The Midrash begins: "I have given you good purchase; forsake not My Torah."[3]

The Midrash proceeds to discuss what a good purchase the Torah is.

> Is there a purchase where the seller is sold along with it? Hashem said to the Jewish people, "I sold you My Torah. As it were, I was sold with it." Thus it is written, *Veyikhu li...,* "They shall take Me...."

The Midrash explains with a parable: A king had an only daughter. A prince from another land married her and when he wanted to return to his land the king told him, "She is my only daughter. I cannot part with her. Nor can I tell you not to take her with you, for she is your wife. Do me a favor. Make me a small room so that I can dwell with you, for I cannot leave my daughter."

Similarly, Hashem said to the Jewish people, "I gave you the Torah. I cannot part with it. Nor can I tell you not to take it. But wherever you go, make me a house so that I can dwell with you." Thus it is written, "They shall me for Me a Sanctuary, and I will dwell among them."[4]

This Midrash is telling us an astounding thing: Hashem, as it were, is found in the Torah! In fact, the *Zohar* says that each word of the Torah is Hashem's Name, and whenever a person learns

---

3. Mishlei 4:2.
4. Shemot 25:8.

Torah, the Shechinah faces him. In other words, Hashem's holiness is in every word of the Torah and connects to each person who learns.

This troubled the angels, who feared that Hashem's honor might be compromised. They immediately stood up for His honor and said, "Place Your glory above the heavens!" — Let the Jewish people have the Torah, but leave Your holiness in heaven.

Moshe countered that the opposite was true. Hashem's honor would be increased if His holiness accompanied the Torah to earth, where men would study it with self-sacrificing devotion amidst the challenges of idolatry, jealousy, and competition.

Moshe won the argument with the angels. The result is that the Torah connects the Jewish people to Hashem; "the Torah, Hashem, and Israel are one." Thus in every era, our Torah giants have Divine inspiration and the blessings they give are fulfilled, for their total devotion to Torah study connects them intensely to Hashem.

Why does the Medrash when expounding our verse, *Veyikhu li terumah,* which is speaking about bringing donations for building the Mishkan,[5] discuss the virtues of the Torah?

Says the Ramban:[6] Hashem's glory, which had rested on Mount Sinai, afterwards rested on the Mishkan. Thus the Torah says, "Hashem's glory rested on Mount Sinai"[7] and "Hashem's glory filled the Mishkan."[8]

So the Mishkan, where Hashem spoke from between the two Keruvim above the Ark, was a continuation of the giving of the Torah at Sinai.

---

5. The portable Tabernacle.
6. Shemot 25:1.
7. Shemot 24:16.
8. Shemot 40:34.

Let's return now to the Midrash, which goes on to explain what a "good purchase" the Torah is:

> Can a person acquire a purchase that is both gold and silver? If it's silver, it isn't gold; and if it's gold, it isn't silver. But the purchase that I have given you has in it silver, as it is written, "Hashem's words are pure words, purified silver,"[9] and it has in it gold, as it is written, "They are more desirable than gold."[10]

This may be understood as follows: Some merchants deal in gold; silver is not worth their while. Others deal in silver; gold is beyond their reach. In Torah, there are scholars who plumb the depths of the Talmud and produce original insights more desirable than gold. And there are men who study plain Halachot and Agadot, which are purified silver. But since they are all Hashem's words, the plain ones can also be enjoyed like gold, and the heavy topics can also be learned in a plain way, like silver.

Finally, the Midrash says that the Torah is a uniquely "good purchase" since it includes both fields and vineyards. That is, the Torah includes parts that are ready to eat, so to speak, like grapes in a vineyard; and parts that are labor-intensive, like wheat in a field. The Torah is for everyone on every level.

A HOUSE FOR HASHEM

They shall make for Me a Sanctuary, and I shall dwell among them.
(Shemot 25:8)

The Midrash[11] relates that when Moshe Rabbenu heard this mitzvah, he wondered how is it possible to build a dwelling place

9. Tehilim 12:7.
10. Tehilim 19:11.
11. *Shemot Rabbah* 34:1.

for Hashem, considering that "He is the place of the world, and the world is not His place." Hashem told him, "It is not as you think. Rather, you will make twenty planks on one side, twenty on the other, and eight there...."

How does this answer Moshe's question?

The Midrash says that Shelomo HaMelech had the same question. Let's examine what Shelomo wrote on the subject.

"Aperion asah lo HaMelech Shelomo, A Temple for His Presence has King Shelomo made of the wood of Lebanon.... Its inside was decked with love by the Jewish people."[12] In other words, the Temple is an expression of the Jewish people's love for Hashem.

To better understand, picture a little boy in kindergarten who made a paper house for his parents. When he brings it home, his mother is delighted. She displays it in the china closet and tells everyone that her son made them a house. Of course, it isn't a house they can live in, but it does express the son's love for his parents. Similarly, the Sanctuary "was inlaid with love by the Jewish people." Of course, no one can build a house for Hashem, but by building the Sanctuary, the Jewish people express their love for Him.

With this we can understand the Gemara:[13]

> There was someone who went around saying, "When our love was strong, both of us could lie on the blade of a knife. But now that our love is not strong, even sixty cubits isn't wide enough for us."
>
> Rav Huna would cite verses to prove this: At first [Hashem said to Benei Yisrael], "I will meet with you there, [and I shall speak with you from atop the Kaporet, from between the two Keruvim that are on the Ark...]."[14]

---

12. *Shir HaShirim* 3:9–10.
13. *Sanhedrin* 7a, as explained by Rashi.
14. Shemot 25:22.

Later on it says, "The House that Shelomo built for Hashem, sixty cubits was its length, twenty is width, and thirty cubits its height."[15]

In the end, it says, "Thus said Hashem: The heaven is My throne, and the earth is My footstool. What House could you build for Me?"[16] [In other words, anything you could build would be too small.]

When people grow accustomed to one another, their love is apt to diminish. But since Hashem doesn't change, as it is written, "I, Hashem, do not change," why does the Gemara compare Hashem's love for us to the person who said, "When our love was strong, both of us could lie on the blade of a knife. But now that our love is not strong, even sixty cubits isn't wide enough for us"?

Obviously, living on a knife blade is not possible in reality, what this person meant was for my part, I would have been willing to do so for love is limitless, but it is restricted by reality. So too, in reality, it is impossible to build a House for Hashem, but through the love in the heart it is perfectly possible, for love is limitless. Thus, through the love the Jewish people had for Hashem they could cause His Presence to dwell amongst them even on the space above the Keruvim. However, as their love diminished so did their capacity to retain His Presence in this space.

Thus at the sea, the Jewish people sang:

> *Zeh Keli ve'anvehu*, "This is my God, and I will build Him a Sanctuary."[17]

They promised to fulfill this mitzvah — which they did not do for any other mitzvah — because building a Sanctuary expresses the Jewish people's love for Hashem. Only with this love can the

---

15. Melachim 1 6:2.
16. Yeshayahu 66:1.
17. As Targum renders.

mitzvah be fulfilled. Without it, anything built would be too small because, "The heaven is My throne, and the earth is my footstool. What House could you build for Me?"

Ve'anvehu has two more meanings:

- I will beautify Myself before Him with mitzvoth; making a beautiful Sefer Torah, beautiful tefillin....
- I will imitate him: Just as He is merciful, so will I be....

All three meanings of *Ve'anvehu* have one underlying theme: they all express the Jewish people's love for Hashem.

The Torah commands: "You shall love Hashem, your God, with all your heart and with all your soul."[18] How is this mitzvah fulfilled? Rambam and Rashi offer two approaches.

Rambam[19] writes that a person "should love Hashem with an exceeding great and strong love until his soul is bound to love of Hashem and he is immersed in it always as one who is lovesick... and even more... as He commanded us, "with all your heart and with all your soul." Thus Shelomo said metaphorically, "I am sick with love,"[20] and all of Shir HaShirim is a metaphor for this.

But Rashi[21] writes: What is the love? [The answer is found in the next verse:] "These words [of Torah study] shall be upon your heart,"[22] for through this you will recognize Hashem and cling to his ways.

Thus according to Rambam, loving Hashem is done by thinking about Him always, but according to Rashi, it is done by learning and fulfilling the Torah and cleaving to His ways. The following story helps resolve the apparent contradiction.

---

18. Devarim 6:5.
19. *Hilchot Teshuvah* 10:3.
20. Shir HaShirim 2:5.
21. On Devarim 6:5, citing *Sifri* 33.
22. Devarim 6:6.

The author of *Ketzot HaHoshen* once visited a Torah scholar. Naturally, they launched into a deep discussion of Torah. But from time to time, an attendant would come in and whisper something in the ear of the Torah scholar. When the *Ketzot* asked why, he replied, "He reminds me to fulfill the Rambam's instructions to think about Hashem always."

Said the *Ketzot,* "You are learning Torah; and since each word of Torah is Hashem's Name, you are connecting to Hashem through learning."

Accordingly, by learning Torah, we fulfill the mitzvah of loving Hashem according to both Rashi and Rambam.

Someone who says he has a desire to learn and know the whole Torah, is not speaking empty words, for even if in reality he can't do it, his words — like building the Sanctuary — express the love in his heart.

THE ARK

They shall make an Ark of acacia wood. (Shemot 25:10)

The Midrash[23] notes that Hashem instructed Bezalel, "You shall make a Table" and "You shall make a Menorah" — but regarding the Ark, He commanded, "They shall make an Ark." Why? Hashem told Moshe, "Let everyone come and involve themselves with the Ark so that all of them will merit Torah."

How exactly were they to involve themselves? Ramban[24] offers three answers: Each Jew would donate a gold vessel especially for the Ark; everyone helped Bezalel a little with its construction; or everyone had special intent for the Ark.

---

23. *Shemot Rabbah* 34:2.
24. Shemot 25:10.

The last point means thinking, "A place for the Torah is being built!" and being happy about it. By eagerly awaiting its completion, a person merits Torah. Similarly, when a yeshiva is built, and we look forward to the time when the Torah will be studied in it, we are connecting to Torah by having intent for it.

The mitzvah of constructing the Mishkan's other furnishings was overseen by Moshe Rabbenu and carried out by Betzalel. But the mitzvah of making the Ark would be fulfilled only if the Jewish people had intent for it, thereby reaccepting the Torah.

This intent went together with prayer.

Both the instructions for making the Ark and those for making the Keruvim above it end with a command to place the Tablets in the Ark.[25] Why the repetition? Perhaps, upon completion, each piece required a different intent and prayer — the Ark, for the flourishing of Torah study and observance; and the Keruvim, which had the faces of children, for the successful transmission of Torah to coming generations.

Now we can understand the Gemara's teaching:[26] If someone tells you, "I toiled but did not find [success]," do not believe him. If he tells you, "I toiled and found," believe him. This refers to words of Torah. But in business, [toiling does not guarantee success, we must rely on] assistance from Above.

The Ark, which represents Torah, requires "toil" — intent and prayer, besides donating money and lending a hand, as the Ramban writes. But the Table, which represents livelihood, depends only on assistance from Above.

---

25. Shemot 25:16,21.
26. *Megillah* 6b.

PARASHAT

Tetzaveh

MOSHE'S NAME IS MISSING

And you shall command Benei Yisrael that they shall take for you pure olive oil... to kindle a lamp continually. (Shemot 27:2)

Baal HaTurim notes that instead of the usual formula — "Hashem spoke to Moshe, saying, 'Command Benei Yisrael'" — here the Torah says, "And you shall command Benei Yisrael." The unusual style continues throughout the Parashah, when Hashem commands Moshe to sanctify Aharon and his sons as Kohanim; to dress them in the priestly garments; and to make the Incense Altar. Moshe's name does not appear once in the entire Parashah. Why? Because when pleading with Hashem to forgive the Jewish people for the golden calf, Moshe had said, "And if not, erase me now from Your Book."[1]

Even though Hashem did grant Moshe's request to forgive them, Moshe's "curse" upon himself was fulfilled, as our Sages taught: A Torah scholar's curse is fulfilled even if it was conditional, regardless of whether the condition was met.[2] The *Zohar*[3] adds: Who is greater than Moshe, who had good reason to say, "And if not, erase me now

---

1. Shemot 32:31.
2. The Rosh writes the same.
3. *Pinhas* 246.

from Your Book"? Yet, he was punished by not having his name mentioned in this Parashah, although Hashem forgave the Jewish people as Moshe wished.

Why specifically this Parasha?

Before answering, let's study the following *Zohar:*[4] Why, in this Parashah, does the Torah repeatedly say, *Ve'atah,* "and you" — *Ve'atah tetzaveh,* "And you shall command... pure olive oil"; *Ve'atah hakrev,* "And you, bring near to yourself Aaron";[5] *Ve'atah tedaber,* "And you shall speak to all the wise of heart"?[6] Because the Shechinah is involved in these matters.

We may explain that all these matters had to be done specifically by Moshe, because of the Shechinah that was with him. Hashem was saying to Moshe: Only you can infuse sanctity into the oil of the Menorah so that the Western Lamp will burn continually, testifying that the Shechinah rests with the Jewish people.[7] Only you can raise Aharon and his sons up out of the Jewish people and make them Kohanim. And only you can recognize the wisdom of the wise of heart.

Only Moshe could do these wonderful things, yet his name was not mentioned and therefore no one appreciated that he did it. He was like one who prepared a splendid banquet for many guests, but didn't get any thanks.

The absence of a name is significant as we see that Yaakov Avinu asked that his name not be mentioned[8] in connection with the evil rebellion of Korah. However, regarding Korah's descendants serving in the Temple, his name was mentioned.[9]

---

4. *Tetzaveh.*
5. Shemot 28:1.
6. Shemot 28:3.
7. See Ramban.
8. See Bereshit 49:6.
9. See Divrei HaYamim 6:22.

The absence of Moshe's name in Parashat Tetzaveh was considered a punishment for Moshe. This was especially so when his name was not mentioned in connection with the oil of the Menorah, for, *Oil and incense gladden the heart*[10] — of Hashem, as Rabbenu Behayei explains. But Hashem is not happy with one who curses himself, as Moshe did.

The Midrash,[11] when describing how Moshe was punished by forfeiting becoming the Kohen Gadol, brings a puzzling parable: A man married his relative and when ten years went by without her bearing any children, he said to her, "I must take another wife. Although I could take one without your permission, please be the one to find me a wife, for I desire your humility." Similarly, when Hashem told Moshe to appoint Aharon as Kohen Gadol, He said to Moshe, "I could have made your brother Kohen Gadol without your knowledge, but I asked you to do it because I want you to be greater than him."

Is appointing one's own successor humility or greatness? Both! The fact that Moshe appointed the Kohanim showed that he was greater than they. But since his name was not mentioned in this connection, it granted him a big boon — a heaping measure of humility.

From this we can learn a powerful lesson. Sometimes a person organizes a *hesed* project or otherwise helps the community but receives no recognition. Instead of grumbling, he should rejoice — for he has just been granted a heaping measure of humility. What could be better? "He has told you... what is good.... to do justice, love kindness, and walk humbly with your God."[12]

Additionally, we see from the boon Moshe received through

---

10. Mishlei 27:9.
11. *Shemot Rabbah* 37:4.
12. Michah 6:8.

his punishment that that there is tremendous compassion along with any punishment that we receive.

GARMENTS OF GLORY

You shall make garments of sanctity for Aaron, your brother, for honor and for splendor. (Shemot 28:2)

If the verse would have said that the garments were honorable and splendid we could understand it. But what is meant by "*for* honor and *for* splendor"?

It means that the garments influenced the wearer to behave in an honorable and dignified way. Similarly, we find in Parashat Bereshit on the verse, "Hashem made for Adam and his wife garments of skin, and He clothed them,"[13] that Targum Onkelos interprets *garments of skin* to mean *garments of honor*.

Thus from the beginning of creation, Hashem gave garments the ability to mold man's character. Our Sages[14] teach us regarding the Kohanim: When the priestly garments are on them, their priesthood is on them; but when they are not wearing them their priesthood is not upon them.

A father once asked a rabbi what to do about his teenage son, who was dirty and sloppy. "Buy him a dignified, expensive hat and suit," said the rabbi.

The father did so, and the garments had their effect, with the son became clean and neat.

Someone once told a Hassidic Rebbe, "Your followers are Hassidic in garb only. Their inside is not like their outside."

The Rebbe replied, "The Mishnah states that if a person makes

---

13. Bereshit 3:21.
14. *Zevahim* 17b.

himself look poor or handicapped, he will not leave this world until he becomes just that. So, too, if my followers make themselves Hassidim on the outside, eventually they will turn into true Hassidim."

There is one condition, however: They must wish to turn into true Hassidim. Only then will the outside have an effect on the inside.

Similarly, when the Gemara[15] speaks of the importance of being thoroughly sincere, it uses the expression *tocho kevaro*, "his inside like his outside." This implies that first the person's outside was in order, and then he worked on aligning his inside with it.

WISDOM OF THE HEART

And you shall speak to all the wise of heart, whom I have filled with a spirit of wisdom... (Shemot 28:3)

What is meant by the "wise of heart"? And if the heart is wise, why does it need to be filled with wisdom?

If we want to understand what a wise heart means, let us look at the wise son in the Pesach Hagadah. He asks, "What are the testimonies, statues, and laws...?" What kind of question is that for a wise son to ask? If he doesn't know the Halachot of Pesach, why is he called wise?

It must be that the wise son is not he who knows, but he who pursues wisdom and wants to know. Such a person is "wise of heart," as in "The wise of heart seizes mitzvot."[16]

---

15. See *Berachot* 28a, *Yoma* 72b.
16. Mishlei 10:8.

This is the exact opposite of Esav. Targum Yonatan[17] states that "Esav was a quiet man" — he didn't ask questions; he wasn't interested in knowing.

It is told that when Rav Eizel Harif was looking for a husband for his daughter, he traveled to the Yeshiva of Volozhin, posed a difficult question in Gemara, and declared that whoever gave the correct answer would become his son-in-law. Many students presented answers, but Rav Eizel refuted them all. It seemed his journey had been in vain.

As he boarded his wagon for the trip home, a student ran after the wagon, shouting, "Rabbi, what's the answer to the question?"

"You will be my son-in-law," said Rav Eizel, "because you want to know the answer."

The wise of heart resembles the wise son in another way as well. The wise son seeks the deep, inner meaning of the mitzvot, and the wise of heart seeks the deep, inner meaning of each matter.

A Hassid once visited the Kotzker Rebbe, who told him, "In Kotzk, we ask questions."

The Hassid couldn't figure out what the Rebbe's statement meant. He asked the elder Hassidim, but received no answer. When he came home, his wife set a meal with bread before him, brought him a cup of water for *netillat yadayim,* and went out for a while.

She came back to find him still holding the cup. He explained, "The Rebbe said that we ask questions, so I asked myself, 'Why do we wash our hands?' I answered, 'Because we are commanded to sanctify ourselves.' Then I asked myself, 'What is this sanctity of the Jewish people all about?'"

---

17. Bereshit 25:27.

In addition to desiring wisdom and seeking the deeper meaning, the wise of heart also fears heaven, as it says, "You shall know this day and take to your heart that Hashem is God... there is none other."[18] The Gemara[19] expounds the verse, "Why is there money [that is, Torah] in the hand of a fool to purchase wisdom, though he has no heart?"[20] — Woe to the scholars who study Torah but have in them no fear of heaven! We see from this, that Fear of heaven is a prerequisite for learning Torah, as our Sages taught,[21] "If a person's fear of sin precedes his wisdom, his wisdom will endure."

But how can we reconcile this with the statement of Rabbi Yanai who said, "Woe to those who don't have a courtyard but make a gate for the courtyard!" And Rashi explains this to mean that the Torah is only a gate by which to come to fear of heaven.

Is fear of heaven the prerequisite or the goal?

The answer is: Both, in an upward spiral. We need to start out with a basic level of fear — that of the "wise of heart," who desires to learn and to know what his duty in this world is. Then the Torah he learns will raise him up to ever higher levels of fear of heaven.

18. Devarim 4:39.
19. *Yoma* 72b.
20. Mishlei 17:16.
21. *Avot* 3:11.

PARASHAT

Ki Tisa

COUNTING THE PEOPLE

When you take the sum of Benei Yisrael according to their numbers, every man shall give Hashem an atonement for his soul when counting them..., so that there will not be a plague among them when counting them. (Shemot 30:12)

Moshe was commanded to take a census by taking a half-shekel from each person. The proceeds were used to buy animals used for public sacrifices.

The Torah states that the rich were not to give more than a half-shekel, nor were the poor to give less.[1] If they did so they would be violating a Torah prohibition according to the Ramban.

Nowhere else do we find such a Torah prohibition. Usually, it is praiseworthy for the rich to give more to charity, and the poor are elsewhere not required to sell the coat off their backs to fulfill a mitzvah, as the Rambam rules they must do for the mizvah of the half shekel.[2] (To fulfill the Rabbinic ordinance of lighting Hanukah lamps, the Rambam rules that one must sell his coat, but does not add "off his back.") Why is the mitzvah of the half-shekel different?

---

1. Shemot 30:15.
2. *Shekalim* 1:1.

116

Another question: The mitzvah of giving half-shekels was given in connection with the census and indeed it was fulfilled when Moshe Rabbenu counted the people through the half-shekels, as recorded in Parashat Bamidbar. Thereafter, the mitzvah of giving a half-shekel was performed yearly without a census. Why, then, was the half-shekel linked to the census the first time?

For that matter, why count the Jewish people at all? Rashi answers that Hashem counted them because they are dear to Him.[3] But this contradicts our Sages' understanding of the verse: "The number of Benei Yisrael will be like the sand of the sea, which can neither be measured nor counted."[4] Our Sages point out that the beginning of the verse says that there is a number, and the end says that there isn't! They explain that when the Jewish people do Hashem's Will they cannot be counted, however, when they don't do Hashem's will, it is possible to count them. If so, why does Rashi say that Hashem counts them because they are dear to Him? When they have a number, they aren't doing His Will!

We can answer all these questions in light of the Ramban's description of how the census was taken: Moshe, Aharon, and the Elders came to each family. The father wrote down his children's names and handed these to Moshe. Moshe looked at them with a good eye, which was a blessing in itself. He blessed them further, saying, "May Hashem... add to you a thousand times yourselves, and bless you as He has spoken of you."[5] Only afterwards did Moshe count the half-shekels.

Why did Moshe personally visit every single family and spend time with them? Evidently, in order to prove that every single Jew is a vital part of the nation. Thus the unique mitzvah of the half-shekel

---

3. See Rashi, Bamidbar 1:1.
4. From the Haftarah of Parashat Bamidbar: Hoshea 2:1.
5. Devarim 1:11.

reinforced the point that every individual was vital. In order that the rich man should not think that he doesn't need others he can only give a half-shekel to show that he is incomplete by himself. And lest the poor man think that he is not needed, he must contribute a half-shekel to the nation even if means selling the coat off his back.

Moshe used the census to unite the Jewish people into a single unit with everyone valuing everyone else. This is Hashem's Will.

If only we would have appreciated the importance of unity, we could have spared ourselves much suffering over the centuries!

In light of this, we can understand why the final redemption will be accompanied by weeping. Hashem says, "With weeping they will come, and through supplications I will bring them...."[6] The Midrash expounds:[7] Just as Yoseph appeased his brothers with weeping, so will Hashem redeem the Jewish people with weeping.

Why will we weep on the day of the redemption? Shouldn't we rather sing for joy?

The answer may be inferred from the Midrash. Our situation resembles that of the brothers, who didn't get along with Yoseph. They hated him on account of his dreams and suspected him of scheming against them. But when they finally met again, they discovered that all the divisiveness had been for nothing. Then they wept, saying, "Why didn't we overcome our differences? We could have spared our father and ourselves so much anguish!"

The Jewish people went into exile because of baseless hatred. When we return from exile, and "the earth will be filled with knowledge of Hashem," we will weep, saying, "Why didn't we overcome our differences? We could have spared ourselves many terrible calamities!"

"The number of Benei Yisrael will be like the sand of the sea."

---

6. Yirmiyahu 31:8.
7. *Bamidbar Rabbah* 93:12.

We have a number when there is dissension among us, which goes against Hashem's Will. But when we are like the number one, which "can neither be measured nor counted," we are doing His Will. The mitzvah of the half- shekel is uniquely stringent because its purpose is uniquely stringent, to unite the Jewish people.

THE SIN OF THE GOLDEN CALF

The people saw that Moshe had delayed in descending from the mountain, and the people gathered against Aharon and said to him, "Arise, make for us a god that will go before us, for this man Moshe who brought us up from the land of Egypt, we know not what became of him." (Shemot 32:1)

Our Sages[8] say: Today the evil inclination tells a person, "Do this," and tomorrow it tells him, "Do that," until finally it tells him, "Go worship idols."

Our Sages are telling us that one comes to idol worship through a gradual process. Yet in this case, the evil inclination skipped all the in-between stages, as the Torah testifies: "They strayed quickly from the way.... They made themselves a molten calf."[9] How did they fall so quickly?

We can ask the same question about Cain. When Hashem rejected his sacrifice, he immediately denied Hashem, saying "There is no justice and there is no judge; there is no reward and no punishment," as Targum Yonatan states. How did Cain fall so quickly?

Evidently the evil inclination has two modes of operation. One is the gradual process, but there is a second mode, where the evil inclination incites a person to anger, and once he is angry he immediately loses his bearings. Our Sages said: Whoever gets

8. *Shabbat* 105b.
9. Shemot 32:8.

angry, his wisdom leaves him. Having lost his logic and reason, he can say and do things that are shocking even to himself once he calms down. Thus, after Hashem rejected Cain's offering it says that "Cain became very angry"[10] — and in his anger, Cain plummeted all the way to denial of Hashem.

The Midrash tells us that the same happened here:[11]

> "The people saw that Moshe had delayed." The Hebrew word for delayed used here is *boshesh* which can be read as *ba'u shesh,*[12] which means that six hours passed from the time he had made up with them, saying, "In forty days, I will bring you the Torah." When six hours passed and Moshe did not descend, immediately "the people gathered against Aharon."

"The people" is the Torah's term for the *erev rav*[13] — Egyptians who had joined the Jewish people out of love for Moshe, who "was very great... in the eyes of Pharaoh's servants."[14] Apparently, before their protector ascended the mountain, they complained about his leaving them; and he promised to return in forty days. When the time came — according to their mistaken calculations — and he did not return, they became angry. Moshe had broken his promise! In their anger, "the people gathered against Aharon and said to him, 'Arise, make for us a god... for this man Moshe who brought us up... we know not what became of him.'"

Anger removes the brakes. An angry person is liable to plummet all the way to idolatry — and even to murder. Thus they killed Hur for rebuking them.

The verse says, "for *this* man Moshe who brought us up from the

10. Bereshit 4:5.
11. *Bereshit Rabbah* 41:7.
12. Literally: six came.
13. Mixed multitude.
14. Shemot 11:3.

land of Egypt, we know not what became of him." Rashi explains that the reason they spoke about *"this* man Moshe" was because Satan showed them an image of Moshe's bier floating in the sky, and they pointed to it. Why was Satan, otherwise known as the evil inclination, given permission to confuse them in this way?

There is a principle that a person is led along the path he wants to take. When one allows himself to become angry, he is choosing to enter a state of confusion. The evil inclination is then given permission to add to his confusion, and he starts imagining things.

Shelomo HaMelech gives us good advice, which I have seen work in difficult situations. "If the ruler's anger flares up against you, do not leave your place"[15] — if the evil inclination brings you to anger, at least don't leave your home. Satan has a way of stirring up anger between husband and wife and between close relatives. If this happens to you, don't run away, for there's no telling where you'll wind up. Instead, bow your head for a while, and soon the storm will pass.

MAKING MERRY

After the Benei Yisrael made the Golden Calf, *They arose early the next day and sacrificed burnt offerings and brought peace offerings. The people sat down to eat and drink, and they got up make merry (letzahek).*[16]

The key term *letzahek* is puzzling. It is related to *tzehok* and *sehok,* both of which mean laughter and playfulness. Sounds harmless? Yet Rashi says that *letzahek* implies immorality and murder;[17] and in fact, they killed Hur.

15. Kohelet 10:4.
16. Shemot 32:6.
17. As proof, he cites Bereshit 39:17 and Shemuel 2 2:14.

What do laughter, playfulness, and merry-making have to do with the cardinal sins?

Besides, the *erev rav* had already killed Hur the previous day, when he rebuked them for wanting to make the golden calf. Now when "they got up *letzahek*," they killed no one — so why does Rashi speak of murder here?

Evidently *letzahek* reveals the character trait that had led to the previous day's murder. On that day, "the people saw that Moshe had delayed in descending the mountain,"[18] on which Targum Yonatan comments that their hearts became flippant.[19] Flippancy knocks down all barriers so that people laugh, scoff, and mock at everything. They hold nothing sacred, not even morality or human life.

No wonder the *Mesilat Yesharim*[20] warns that being immersed in merriment and frivolity is like drowning in the ocean! The Mishnah[21] also warns that these lead to immorality.

Moreover, says the *Mesilat Yesharim*,[22] one jest repels a hundred reproofs; it's like a shield smeared with oil, which deflects all arrows shot at it. Thus the *erev rav* were unable to accept Hur's reproof and get back on course.

Interestingly, the ashes of the *parah adumah*,[23] atoned for the sin of the golden calf. The Midrash[24] compares the matter to a maidservant whose son dirtied the king's palace; people said, "Let his mother come and clean her son's excrement." Similarly, the heifer came and atoned for the calf.

18. Shemot 32:1.
19. *Zehuhin.*
20. Chapters 2,5.
21. *Avot* 3:17.
22. Chapters 2,5.
23. Red heifer.
24. On Bamidbar 19:22.

The Midrash may be understood as follows. The maidservant must clean the palace to teach her how severe it is to dirty the king's palace. Similarly, because they were immersed in merriment and frivolity, the *erev rav* did not realize how severe it was to make a golden calf, and they had to learn this through the *parah adumah*. This mitzvah requires the opposite of frivolity, it requires so much contemplation that even the wisest of men, Shelomo HaMelech, felt it was beyond his grasp and said, "I thought I could become wise, but it is beyond me."[25]

The lesson for us is to keep away from frivolous merriment and adopt the trait of *zehirut*[26] — carefully considering our deeds before we do them, and reviewing them afterwards. At all times, we must be aware that we are in the presence of the King.

MOSHE'S PLEA

[After the sin of the Golden Calf, Moshe pleaded,] *"And now, if only You would forgive their sin! But if not, erase me now from Your Book that You have written."*

Hashem said to Moshe, "He who has sinned against Me shall I erase from My book." (Shemot 32:32–33)

Rashi explains that *Your Book* refers to the whole Torah, thus Moshe was saying that if Hashem would not forgive their sin, he wanted his name removed from the Torah. Ramban objects: If this is so, how can we explain Hashem's answer, "He who has sinned against Me shall I erase from My book"? No one else could be erased from His Book, since the sinners hadn't been recorded in the Torah to begin with!

---

25. Kohelet 7:23.
26. Literally: carefulness.

We may answer this question in light of our Sages' teaching that there are six hundred thousand letters in the Torah, corresponding to the six hundred thousand souls of the Jewish people. That is, each Jewish soul has a corresponding letter in the Torah. Accordingly, Hashem was saying: Those who worshiped the golden calf, thereby desecrating the Torah's commands, will lose their connection to their letter in the Torah.

Rashi explains that Moshe made this unusual request so that they would not say of him that he was unworthy of pleading for mercy for them. But why was Moshe concerned with what people would say?

We may answer in light of what our Sages[27] taught that a person who has a sick family member should ask a Torah scholar to pray for mercy. The *Nimukei Yoseph* adds that the custom in France was to ask a rosh yeshiva to bless the sick person. People will only do so if they believe the tzaddik has the power to evoke Divine compassion. Moshe was worried that if he failed, they would not believe in the power of a tzaddik's prayer, and would not avail themselves of his prayers. As always, Moshe Rabbenu was not concerned for himself, but for his fellow Jews.

---

27. *Bava Batra* 116a.

PARASHAT

Vayakhel

THE MISHKAN AND SHABBAT

Moshe assembled the entire congregation of Benei Yisrael and said to them: ...The seventh day shall be holy for you, a complete Shabbat for Hashem; whoever does work on it shall be put to death. You shall not kindle fire... on the Shabbat day. (Shemot 35:1–3)

Rashi notes that Moshe delivered this warning about Shabbat before the command to build the Mishkan, to teach that building the Mishkan does not supersede the Shabbat. Rashi made a similar remark in Parashat Ki Tisa,[1] where Shabbat is mentioned after the command to make the Mishkan, its furnishings, and the priestly garments.

Why was it necessary to warn the Jewish people twice? Besides, why would they have thought to work on the Mishkan on Shabbat?

The people might have thought that working on the Mishkan, is considered involvement in Shabbat — since in essence, the Mishkan and Shabbat are the same.

The *Zohar*[2] teaches us that blessing rested on the Table in the Mishkan, and from it sustenance went out to the whole world.

---

1. Shemot 31:13.
2. *Terumah* 153b.

The Ramban[3] writes that the blessing of sustenance came particularly through the *Lehem HaPanim*.[4] For blessing cannot appear in a vacuum, it must begin from something that already exists, as we see from Elisha who performed a miracle for the destitute widow of the prophet Ovadiah. He had her pour oil into many empty containers, miraculously filling them all. However, he could not do so until she had some oil of her own. Note that new *Lehem HaPanim* was set out on the Table every Shabbat.

And Shabbat is also the source of all blessing as it says, "God blessed the seventh day,"[5] which the *Zohar*[6] explains to mean that all bounty that will descend from heaven to earth in the coming six days descends on Shabbat. Similar to the Table in the Mishkan, our Shabbat table in particular, is the source of blessing and we set food on it and eat three meals, because blessing needs to rest and start from something.

A look at the psalm of Shabbat, *Mizmor shir leyom HaShabbat*,[7] will help us understand this.

> It is good to thank Hashem… for You have gladdened me, Hashem, with your works.… How great are Your deeds, Hashem; your thoughts are very deep. A *baar*[8] man does not know.…

What exactly is "a *baar* man"? Elsewhere, *baar* refers to grazing livestock.[9] Animals eat without thinking, and a *baar* man does the same. Man is meant to think — to contemplate Hashem's awesome works. This is especially true at the Shabbat table,

3. Shemot 22:24.
4. Showbread.
5. Bereshit 2:3.
6. Shemot 89.
7. Tehilim 92.
8. Commonly translated: boorish.
9. Parashat Mishpatim: Shemot 22:4.

which is the source of blessing. We sample Hashem's creation on Shabbat in order to connect with Him by enjoying His products. This brings down blessing; as David HaMelech said, "Delight in Hashem, and He will grant you your heart's wishes."[10]

A rabbi once told his guest, "I would like to say a *hiddush*[11] about Shabbat" — and launched into a discussion of watermelons. He enthused over how the sweet, juicy, edible part is red, in order to draw the eye, while the inedible part which serves as protective packaging, is white and hard. Noticing the surprise on his guest's face, he explained, "The psalm of Shabbat says, 'How great are Your deeds, Hashem; your thoughts are very deep.'"

The blessing brought down through the table is not the only parallel between the Mishkan and Shabbat. In the Mishkan, the sacrifices atoned for us; on Shabbat, Kiddush and the Shabbat meal atones for us, as the Gemara[12] says, "When a man makes Kiddush, two ministering angels place their hands on his head and say, 'Your iniquity shall depart, and your sin shall be atoned.'"

The Mishkan contained the Ark with the Tablets, and the Menorah, symbolizing the light of Torah. Shabbat was given for Torah study. Whoever learns Torah on Shabbat will see much success in his learning during the coming week.

The Mishkan was a spiritual world, and so is Shabbat. When we enter the holiness of Shabbat, we receive a *neshamah yeterah*,[13] and we should feel in a different realm, a spiritual world, the world of the soul.

Shabbat is a semblance of the world to come. It reminds us that we are in this world in order to prepare for the next one, with

---

10. Tehilim 37:4.
11. Original Torah insight.
12. *Shabbat* 119b.
13. Additional soul.

this lesson reinforced weekly. We know that we will enjoy delicacies on Shabbat only if we shop, cook, and bake during the week; this should remind us that we will enjoy the reward of the world to come only if we learn Torah and do mitzvot now in this world.

On Shabbat, unless we turn on lights beforehand, we will sit in the dark. "A mitzvah is a candle, and the Torah is light";[14] if we don't want to sit in the dark in the world to come, we must do mitzvot here — with intent to do Hashem's Will, along with joy and awe.

According to Ramban,[15] it is a mitzvah of the Torah to remember Shabbat every day of the week; thus we say, "Today is the first [or: second, third...] day to Shabbat." Similarly, throughout our lives we must remember that we are here to prepare for "the day that is wholly Shabbat."

These two aspects of Shabbat — bringing material and spiritual blessing for the next week, and reminding us of the world to come — are reflected in the two versions of the Ten Commandments. The first Tablets said, "Remember the Shabbat day to sanctify it.... For in six days Hashem made the heavens, the earth, the sea and all that is in them."[16] Remembering Shabbat corresponds to the idea of, "How great are Your works, Hashem," which enables us to bring down blessing for the coming week. The second Tablets said, "Safeguard the Shabbat day."[17] This commands us to refrain from cooking, baking, and all the other *melachot*;[18] which insures that we prepare for Shabbat in advance. This, in turn, encourages us to prepare for the world to come.

How fortunate we Jews are! All the laws of Shabbat bring

---

14. Mishlei 6:23.
15. Shemot 20:8.
16. Shemot 20:8–11.
17. Devarim 5:12.
18. Forbidden types of "work."

us tremendous benefit. "More than the Jewish people safeguard Shabbat, Shabbat safeguards them."[19]

BETZALEL

Moshe said to Benei Yisrael, saying, "See, Hashem has called [to lead in the construction of the Mishkan] by name, Betzalel son of Uri son of Hur.... He has filled him with a Godly spirit...."[20]

Earlier, the Torah said:

Hashem said to Moshe, saying, "See, I have called by name Betzalel son of Uri son of Hur.... I have filled him with a Godly spirit...."[21]

Why did Moshe tell Benei Yisrael of Israel to "see," and why did Hashem tell the same to Moshe? What exactly needed to be seen?

We may answer the first question in light of the Midrash,[22] which relates that the Jewish people complained about nepotism, for Betzalel's grandfather, Hur was the son of Moshe's sister, Miriam.[23] Moshe told them that it was not he who had chosen Betzalel, but Hashem. Says the Midrash: Moshe pointed and said, "See, Hashem has called by name, Betzalel."

What did Moshe point to that proved that Betzalel was chosen by Hashem?

I suggest that he pointed to the Ark, for its powerful sanctity proved that Hashem had bestowed sanctity on its builder. Thus on the verse "Betzalel made the Ark,"[24] the Midrash[25] says: He was

---

19. *Kuzari.*
20. Shemot 35:30–31.
21. Shemot 31:1 –2.
22. Tanhuma 3.
23. Who had married Calev.
24. Shemot 37:1.
25. *Tanhuma 7.*

called Betzalel, which means "In the Shade of Hashem", because he made the two Keruvim, which shaded with their wings for Hashem, as it is written, "I will speak with you... from between the two Keruvim that are on the Ark."[26]

The Midrash continues: The whole Mishkan was made only for the Ark, in which the Shechinah rested. There were many miracles wrought for the Jewish people through the Ark as it is written, "The Ark of the Covenant of Hashem journeyed a three-day distance before them to search out a resting place for them."[27] Two sparks emerged from between the two Keruvim to kill snakes and scorpions, burn thorns, and slay enemies. At that time, Moshe would say, "Arise, Hashem, and let Your foes be scattered...."[28]

Thus Moshe said to the people, "See [the Ark! It proves that] Hashem has called Betzalel by name" — the miracles of the Ark are possible only because Hashem chose Betzalel and gave him tremendous sanctity and heavenly assistance.

We have explained why Moshe told the people, "See," but we must still explain why Hashem told Moshe, "See".

We may answer in light of the following Gemara:[29] Betzalel was named for his wisdom. When Hashem told Moshe, "Go tell Betzalel to make Me a Mishkan, an Ark, and furnishings," Moshe reversed the order telling Betzalel, "Make furnishings, an Ark, and a Mishkan."

"Moshe Rabbenu," said Betzalel, "the way of the world is that a person builds a house and then puts furnishings in it. Yet you tell me, 'Make furnishings, an Ark, and a Mishkan.' Where will I put the furnishings that I make? Did Hashem perhaps say, 'Make a Mishkan, an Ark, and furnishings'?"

26. Shemot 25:22.
27. Bamidbar 10:33.
28. Bamidbar 10:35.
29. *Berachot* 55a.

"Yes," said Moshe. "Were you in the shade of Hashem that you knew this?"

Accordingly, Hashem told Moshe to *see* for himself Betzalel's wisdom. Moshe therefore tested Betzalel by reversing the order, and Betzalel passed the test.

Betzalel's argument is puzzling on two counts. He asked about the order of building the Mishkan based on "the way of the world." Why should the Mishkan be built according to the way of the world? Secondly, he asked, "Where will I put the furnishings that I make?" Even though the Mishkan was constructed first, it would wait, covered in curtains, for three months — from Kislev, when it was completed, until Nissan, when it was assembled. So, in any case, the furnishings were not put into the Mishkan immediately. And Betzalel surely knew this through Divine inspiration.

Perhaps the wise Betzalel spoke of "the way of the world" and asked, "Where will I put the furnishings that I make?" because he deduced that the Torah when building the Mishkan wanted to teach us the purpose of a house.

There are people who think that a house is to show off to the street. They decorate the exterior grandly and call attention to it at night with spotlights. But the Torah teaches us that our house is a place to "put the furnishings." It's a place to shelter us and our belongings.

Rabbi Yaakov Galinsky related that he once saw a man decorating the outside of his house grandly. Rabbi Galinsky went over to him and said, "I think you should put the flowers on the right and the grass on the left, and paint the gate green."

"Who asked for your opinion?" asked the man.

"You did," said Rabbi Galinsky. "I see that you're decorating to impress me, so I'm telling you what will impress me."

How did Betzalel deduce that the outside of a house should be modest and not attract attention? From the fact that in contrast to the magnificent silver and gold inside, the Mishkan's exterior was to be singularly unimpressive; it was made of goatskin. Betzalel therefore said, "Although the Ark and the furnishings will not go into the Mishkan now, we will make them in a certain order, to teach all generations that a house is for sheltering its occupants and containing their furnishings, not for attracting attention."

Thus on the verse "Betzalel made the Ark," the Midrash[30] says: "You find that everything in the Mishkan was made in a certain order." The Torah describes that order at length in order to teach us how to build our home.

---

30. *Tanhuma* 10.

PARASHAT

Pikudei

THE PRIESTLY GARMENTS ATONED

They made the holy garments for Aaron, as Hashem commanded Moshe.
(Shemot 39:1)

The Gemara[1] states that the garments of the Kohen Gadol atoned like the sacrifices. The *kutonet* — shirt atoned for bloodshed; the *michnasayim* — pants, for immorality; the *hoshen* — breastplate for miscarriage of justice; the *me'il* — tunic, for *lashon hara*....

How did the priestly garments atone for the Jewish people? First, let's understand how garments affect the wearer.

When the prophet Shemuel was little, "his mother would make him a small robe and bring it to him from year to year."[2] We don't need a verse to tell us that Hannah clothed her son; every mother does that. Rather, the verse is telling us that Hannah put tremendous love for Hashem and sanctity into this robe, which influenced Shmuel when he wore it.

Similarly, special thoughts and intentions, including fear of particular sins, were put into each garment of the Kohen Gadol, "as Hashem commanded Moshe." These influenced the Kohen Gadol, elevating him to great spiritual heights and intensifying his

---

1. *Arachin* 16a.
2. Shemuel 1 1:19.

fear of sin. From him, fear of sin spread to all the Jewish people.

The story is told of a village Hassid who requested his Rebbe's permission to move to the big city. "There are many God-fearing people in the city," explained the Hassid.

"Are there any in your village?" asked the Rebbe.

"There is one who fears Hashem greatly," replied the Hassid.

"Then stay where you are and cleave to him," said the Rebbe. "His fear of Hashem will affect you, for fear is contagious. We learn this from the announcement made to Jewish soldiers: 'Who is the man who is fearful...? He shall go and return to his house, and not melt his brothers' hearts'[3] — if he stays, his fear will spread from one to another until it infects the entire army."

This explains how the garments of the Kohen Gadol atoned.

Wearing the priestly garments lifted the Kohen Gadol to pinnacles of fear of sin. His fear radiated out to the Kohanim around him, and their fear spread to others, until everyone repented and was forgiven.

From the Kohen Gadol, we learn that a single individual can affect the whole world. Says the Gemara:[4] Great is repentance; the entire world is forgiven for the sake of one person who repents. As proof, the Gemara cites the verse "I will heal their waywardness, I will love them gratuitously, for My anger has turned away from him."[5] Note that it does not say "from them," rather, "from him" — because of one person who repents.

Of course, sinners must scour their own soul to restore its original whiteness, as *Shaarei Teshuvah*[6] says, but another person's repentance can remove the outer layer of grime.

---

3. Devarim 20:8.
4. *Yoma* 86b.
5. Hoshea 14:5.
6. 1:9.

In practical terms, this means that if one of us observes Shabbat with greater enthusiasm, a non-observant Jew somewhere in the world will refrain from converting to a different faith.

REPETITION

Moshe saw the entire work, and behold, they had done it as Hashem had commanded... and Moshe blessed them. (Shemot 39:43)

After summarizing the construction of the Mishkan's elements here, the Torah relates that the Mishkan was erected and the Shechinah came to rest on it. Thus ends Humash Shemot.

We might well wonder, the Torah after detailing the instructions for the construction of the Mishkan and the Preistly vestments in Parashat Terumah and Titzaveh, repeats in detail their actual construction in Parashat Vayakhel and Pikudei. Couldn't the Torah have sufficed with the short summary of our verse?

To explain the repetition, let us study a Midrash[7] that connects the phrase, "As Hashem commanded Moshe,"[8] in our Parashah, with the phrase, "He called to Moshe," at the opening of Humash Vayikra

The Midrash brings a parable of a king who told his servant, "Build me a palace." On every part the servant built, he wrote the king's name. When building the walls, he wrote on them the king's name and when building the ceilings, he wrote the king's name.

When the king entered the palace and saw his name wherever he looked, he said, "My servant accorded me all this honor — yet I am inside while he is outside? Call him and let him enter the innermost chamber!"

---

7. *Vayikra Rabbah* 1:7.
8. Shemot 40:32 and many other verses.

Similarly, Hashem said to Moshe, "Make me a Mishkan," and
on every part that Moshe made, he wrote "as Hashem commanded
Moshe." Hashem said, "Moshe accorded Me all this honor — and
I am inside while he is outside? Call him and let him enter the
innermost chamber!" Thus it is written, "He called to Moshe."

Moshe surely did not actually write "as Hashem commanded
Moshe," for it was forbidden to deviate from Hashem's instruction. How are we to understand the Midrash?

It is told that Rabbi Isser Zalman Meltzer knew whether a
utensil had undergone *tevilat kelim*[9] just by looking at it. If he saw
Hashem's Name right side up on the utensil, he knew that the
utensil had been immersed; if he saw the Name upside down, it
had not been.

Our Sages teach that the walls of a person's house testify about
him in the world to come. This means that his deeds, good or bad,
are recorded on them. Evidently they are also recorded on his car,
for Rabbi Yisrael Abuhatzera once refused to get into a car that
had been sent for him, because its owner drives it on Shabbat.

On the positive side, the Ben Ish Hai[10] taught that any physical object that serves holiness acquires some holiness itself. Thus
the prophet's staff, on which he would lean while thinking holy
thoughts, acquired sanctity; and our Sages compared the rock on
which Rabbi Eliezer ben Horkenos sat while studying Torah, to
Mount Sinai.

In short, when a person fulfills a mitzvah in holiness and pu-
rity in order to fulfill Hashem's Will, the objects he uses acquire
sanctity, and Hashem's Name appears on them. This certainly
applied to the Mishkan, which was constructed under Moshe's

---

9. Ritual immersion of utensils made by 1or acquired from a gentile.
10. *Ben Yehoyada, Sanhedrin* 95a.

supervision and finally erected by him. The Torah records that each part was made "as Hashem commanded Moshe" to tell us that Hashem's Name appeared on each part — a great honor to Him.

This accounts for some but not all of the repetition. The Torah not only records in detail the instructions for making the Mishkan and the fact that the Jews made each part, but also that they brought the various parts to Moshe, and that Moshe put each part in its place.

We may find an explanation in the *Daat Zekenim* and the Rosh, who wrote:

> How precious was the Mishkan! For it corresponded to the creation of the world!
>
> On the first day, Hashem created the heavens, "spreading out the heavens like a curtain;"[11] in the Mishkan, they made curtains of goatskin.
>
> On the second day, He made the firmament as a divider; in the Mishkan, they made the *Parochet* as a divider.
>
> On the third day, He gathered the waters; in the Mishkan, they gathered water in the *Kiyor*.
>
> On the fourth day, He made the luminaries; in the Mishkan, they made the gold Menorah.
>
> On the fifth day, He created the birds; in the Mishkan, they made winged Keruvim.
>
> On the sixth day, He created man; in the Mishkan, Aharon was drawn close.
>
> On the seventh day, Hashem's creation was completed; and our Parashah says, "All the work of the Mishkan was completed."[12]

---

11. Tehilim 104:2.
12. Shemot 39:32.

To us, the verses about the Mishkan appear repetitious, but apparently they were needed for creating and directing the world. For, as our Sages put it, "He looked into the Torah and created the world" — the Torah is the blueprint of the universe.